Yet Alive? Methodists in British Fiction since 1890

Yet Alive? Methodists in British Fiction since 1890

By

David Dickinson

Cambridge
Scholars
Publishing

Yet Alive? Methodists in British Fiction since 1890

By David Dickinson

This book first published 2016. The present binding first published 2016.

Cambridge Scholars Publishing

Lady Stephenson Library, Newcastle upon Tyne, NE6 2PA, UK

British Library Cataloguing in Publication Data
A catalogue record for this book is available from the British Library

ISBN (10): 1-4438-0294-8
ISBN (13): 978-1-4438-0294-9

To Yvette

whose interest in this project has been a constant encouragement

I am not afraid that the people called Methodists should ever cease to exist either in Europe or America. But I am afraid lest they should only exist as a dead sect, having the form of religion without the power. And this undoubtedly will be the case unless they hold fast both the doctrine, spirit, and discipline with which they first set out.
'Thoughts Upon Methodism,' John Wesley 1786

The Methodist Church … stands for the best traditions of liberal, socially committed Christianity. It is a Church that encourages people to think, rather than force-feeding them with instant answers. There are plenty of people in contemporary society who are searching for meaning in their lives, suspicious of certainty, but deeply interested in the spiritual dimension. Perhaps the Methodist Church needs to be more serious about being true to its own nature, about exploring new ways of relating to people in their spiritual search, rather than giving in to the temptation to emulate churches which generally take a more conservative stance.
'Gone But Not Forgotten,' p. 96

TABLE OF CONTENTS

ACKNOWLEDGEMENTS

The words on these pages have been written with a sense of gratitude to the Right Reverend Geoffrey Rowell who commissioned the article on Methodism in English fiction that developed into this book, William Gibson of Oxford Brookes University and the Wesley Centre, Oxford at Westminster Institute of Education who permitted access to its archives in November 2011, Peter Hobbs who discussed his novel with me, Michael Chaplin who discussed his father's life and work with me, Catherine Meredith (Houses of Parliament librarian) and the staff of the parliamentary archives. My editor, Dr. Gladys Lewis, has worked her magic on the words I originally put on the page and made them worthy of publication: I am so deeply grateful for the criticism she offers in such an affirming way. Thanks, too, to scholars I have worked with over the years who have helped nudge doors open so that my work can be shared. Greatest of all, though, is my gratitude to the Methodist people alongside whom I have worshipped and among whom I have worked as a minister for thirty years.

PREFACE

Theology means God-talk, a word that many Christian believers find off-putting because it smacks of the intellectualisation of individual emotion, experience and belief and locates thought about God in academia. Except when expressed through music or visual arts, theology uses words to communicate itself. Although recognisably inadequate, language is the usual medium to express ultimacy, infinity and ineffability. Theology equals words about God.

Literature is also a verbal art. Poetry and prose rely on words, and their creators use language to construct their art, express their ideas, and tell their stories. That both theology and literature employ words brings them into irresistible symbiosis, such that I find it impossible to live as a Christian and work as a Christian minister without thinking about God through literature. Over thirty years ago I left a career teaching secondary school English to become a Methodist minister, so my work has lived out the theology-literature symbiosis. When my work was to teach English, at the tail end of the 1970s and the first half of the 1980s, some of the writers discussed in this text were on the curriculum—Chaplin's *The Leaping Lad* was regarded as accessible for school children in the West End of Newcastle upon Tyne—and, at weekends, I served as a local preacher in the chapels that writers such as J. L. Carr, Arthur Quiller-Couch and Sheila Kaye-Smith would have instantly recognised. Within a few years of full-time ministry, I was in touch with a fellow Methodist, a scholar famed for his study of English hymnody, Richard Watson, then of Durham University. I had a query, the subject of which I cannot remember. In the course of our conversation, I shared my "grass is always greener on the other side" conundrum. When I taught English, I loved theology; now that I was a theologian (for that is what clergy people are), my love of literature burgeoned. He invited me to attend the 1992 annual conference of the International Society for Religion and Literature as an observer in Glasgow. Listening to theologians discuss literature and literary scholars discuss theology hooked me in. I have lived in the territory shared by theology and literature ever since. Nowadays, when I read a novel, I am doing theology.

Literature, the primary subject of this text, occupies a significant part of the modern church where words fill the air when we worship, to such an extent that some crave silence. When Christian believers congregate on their day of worship, they gather around a book to hear its word proclaimed that they may discover in its words the Word who spoke the world into being. That this book forms the Christian scriptures emphasises that it has been written, for the word "scripture" is obviously associated with terms such as "script" and "manuscript." Written by whom? Written by men—disturbingly so for women in a less patriarchal society—who believed they were in some way recording, not only words about God (theology), but the words *of* God. Many who read it today read it to listen for the authentic divine voice. Moreover, the worship offered when Christians gather in churches uses a particular form of poetry in its formal prayers, hymnody and carefully crafted language, sometimes crafted over the course of centuries. The preacher engages his or her rhetorical art in the oratory of the sermon—again, words. In addition to this inevitable literary focus of worship, practical theology in that it expresses what Christians believe about God, I, in common with many other worship leaders, sometimes include non-biblical texts alongside Bible readings and, like many other preachers, frequently allude to literature in sermons. The stories and scenes of novels, lines of poetry and plots of TV dramas, films and theatre fund many a contemporary sermon. Much more than using literature for sermon illustration, this can entail genuine and deep dialogue between the disciplines of theology and literature, thereby enriching the human perception of the divine. The Catholic hymn "*Ubi Caritas*" and Leo Tolstoy's much-loved story of Martin the Cobbler teach that, where love is, God is. I have learnt that where literature and theology, my two loves, converge God is also found.

Born into a Methodist family, I am, however, a Methodist by conviction. I believe its distinctive theology, outlined in chapter one, brings an important contribution to the panoply of contemporary Christianity, and *Yet Alive?* progresses naturally from my years of study, thought and practice in the field of religion and literature. Part of a continuing exploration of the interface between the two disciplines, I have been keen to discover how fiction, a branch of literature, depicts Methodism, one of the larger Protestant groupings within Christianity, yet still much smaller and less influential than the Orthodox and Catholic Churches.

Every reader reads with pre-understanding, so when I read novels I hold several assumptions. Decades of wide-ranging fiction reading has developed within me a high doctrine of fiction, and I have high expectations of any novel I hold in my hands. I am almost persuaded that prose fiction can achieve more than any other literary form. Novels can capture the least definable aspects of my experience in life and leave me marvelling at the mystery of it all. They are so open and flexible in form that they can host more than one worldview, exist on several planes at once, and place me, if I allow them, wherever they want. Such is the creative power of novels. Novels embody characteristics of the cultures in which their narratives are set and in which their authors live, and can also hint at another reality beyond; they can mix reality and irreality; they can mix magic and realism; they can speak of things seen and unseen; they can deal with the tangible, quotidian world and offer traces and glimpses of another higher world and higher Being. Novels are tangible yet transcendent. For this reason, my indebtedness to fiction in my formation and practice as a Christian minister is inexpressible. Reading a novel lifts me to another plane and helps me gain alternative perspectives on all that meets the eye.

Unlike theology, which uses reasonable argument in its striving for orderliness and understanding, fiction is rarely neat. In its messy depiction of human relationships, it mirrors the twists and turns I and others take on our way through life. As a result, the interdependence of literature and theology finds creative tension in the case of fiction. The tendency of theology to systematise and the capacity of fiction to contain inconsistencies establish a tension of different expectations from which fresh understandings of human existence can emerge. This accounts for what I sometimes think is a misperception of a "sacred turn" in British novels since the 1980s. Novels have always been able to speak of remarkable or marvellous things (to borrow part of the title of Jon McGregor's 2002 debut novel, in which an anonymous city street becomes a miraculous place). The convergence of sacred and secular in fiction is no recent phenomenon, but, rather, a continuation of the way fiction has always presented itself. Perhaps contemporary readers pick up on the implied presence of the spiritual in novels because they engage less with organised religion, thus signifying a sacred turn among readers instead of a sacred turn in novels. In my own preaching and writing, I have found the tension between literature and theology both a helpful discipline, in that theology has reined me in from chasing seductive unorthodox thoughts up theological cul-de-sacs, and creative, in that literature has restrained theology's tendency towards dogmatism and permitted exploration. Living and working within the territory shared by literature and theology has enabled me to push at the edges and forge new expressions of Christianity's old, old story for the current age in order to tell the gospel afresh.

When I read, I also assume that I am not reading alone. The act of reading appears solitary. Readers shut out distractions, turn their gaze from whatever occurs around them and immerse themselves in a book. Yet we read in company, not alone. First, we read with the author and his or her characters; we dialogue with them. And we also read with other readers (usually implicitly but sometimes explicitly if we will later meet in a book club to discuss our reading). To this end, I have set up church book clubs. How much they have contributed to my study of Methodism in fiction is difficult to gauge for I have learnt from other readers over many years. Moreover, we read the novel we presently have in our hands with memories of books we have previously read and their authors. And we read the book in our hands in dialogue with our experience of the culture we live in. These form interpretive communities and prevent isolated reading. Communal reading holds our individualistic views in check and keeps us in good company. I can imagine a congregation of readers. As I write, I imagine a company of Methodists reading of themselves and their forebears, and I am among them.

INTRODUCTION

The governing body of the Methodist Church in Britain, the Methodist Conference, meets annually, opening its proceedings with the *a cappella* singing of Charles Wesley's hymn "And are we yet alive and see each other's face?" Seemingly amazed that they have survived another gruelling year, Conference representatives raise their voices in song. That the hymn begins with the word "and" introduces an element of astonishment, implying also that its singers are part way through a conversation which presumably began at some undetermined point in the years of fervent activity between 1738, when the Wesley brothers experienced separate heart-warming experiences, and 1744, when the first collection of Charles Wesley's hymns was published. Further, the "and" signals continuation as long as Methodists live. Throughout this conversation, literary interest in the Methodist movement has been shown, beginning surprisingly early in that, within ten years of the beginning of the Wesley brothers' public ministry, Henry Fielding subjected the movement to literary scrutiny in his novels. A significant turning point in this literary interest in Methodism occurred in 1890 with the publication of Harold Frederic's *The Damnation of Theron Ware*, and this forms the starting point of this study. Surprisingly, the denomination, highly controversial at its inception, in steep decline since the First World War and struggling currently with its sense of identity, still features in British literature, so "Yet alive?" serves as a fitting title for a study of Methodists in British fiction in the last hundred years.

In 2014, the year of the preparatory work for this book, the President of Conference, the Reverend Dr. Kenneth Howcroft, used his presidential address to ask in his opening paragraph, and answer, what some might regard as a dangerous question: What is Methodism for? Posing this question in such a public arena can be seen as bringing into the open a crisis of confidence: Are we yet alive? What is the purpose of Methodism? Has it anything to offer British society and individuals within it? This text examines novels that, in various ways and to differing degrees, have asked similar questions. They have explored the contribution Methodism has made to the spiritual lives, the religious landscape, and the theological understanding of the British reading public; cumulatively, they have established a portrait of the denomination in the popular imagination.

Contemporary Methodists will want to consider whether the portrait presented in fiction proves accurate, misleading or, indeed, complete enough to be worthwhile.

Since 1940, when T. B. Shepherd published *Methodism and the Literature of the Eighteenth Century,*[1] a hiatus in this field of study has existed, and there has been little scholarly interest in Methodism's literary portrait in the twentieth century. Almost all publications concerning Methodism in literature have been restricted to the literature of the eighteenth and nineteenth centuries. Most of these have considered the influence of Methodism either on the writers or their novels; some have assessed the literary contribution of celebrated Methodist novelists; some have looked for Methodist traits and themes in well-known fiction of the century, such as that of the Brontës and George Eliot's celebrated depiction of Methodism. But all ended their studies at the close of what some historians call "the long nineteenth century", dating it from the French Revolution of 1789 to the outbreak of World War One in 1914. All regarded the literary analysis as a means of studying the historical Methodist movement, and many were written from an American perspective or for a specifically American market. This book covers, approximately, the next hundred years from 1914 to the present. In asking how the denomination is portrayed in fiction, this examination approaches the subject from a decidedly literary perspective. Its main interest lies in how the denomination has been described and discussed in novels rather than how it has influenced them. Inevitably, therefore, this book offers a critique of some neglected and forgotten novels, perhaps assisting in the recovery of some of these authors from the obscurity that results unjustifiably from the fads and fancies of literary fashion.

Recovery of neglected authors would be a felicitous by-product, but this book's primary purposes are three-fold. First, it attempts to fill the gap left since Shepherd closed his work. Secondly, it should add, in a small way, to the assessment of the role of religion in British literature, which continues to host spiritual, religious and theological themes despite being written and read in an age of competing convictions of faith and belief. Thirdly, it contributes to Methodist studies in that it analyses the more recent depiction in literature of the denomination's people, origins, ecclesiology and theology which has escaped published scholarly description, except for this author's article of 2013, *Methodism in English Fiction.*[2] Readers who are familiar with Methodism and its history will profit from the review offered herein. Non-Methodist adherents will learn that narrative. Both groups will profit from new insights that will come from the literary depiction of a valued religious orientation.

In the nineteenth century, many novels found their framing with Methodist settings, themes, characters and authors, some of which will be discussed as background in the second chapter. Many of these were highly successful in publishing terms. Indeed, the first novelist to sell a million copies of one title in Britain was a Methodist minister, Silas Hocking, whose *Her Benny* of 1879 told a story of street children who were abused by their parents and sold matches for a living. Based on his experiences as a minister in Liverpool, it outsold the works of much better-remembered writers of the time.[3] He and his siblings, Joseph and Salome Hocking, wrote their novels, documenting the ideas and ideals of Methodism, with the express intention of making their beliefs accessible to a wider audience and converting them to the Methodist cause. Unapologetically didactic and propagandistic, the Hockings were romanticists who wrote of a Methodism that never existed and of Methodists dreaming of conversions they never got.[4] In contrast with the Hockings' hagiographical style, most nineteenth-century novels dismissed Methodism as a distasteful or hypocritical sect whose zealous, and sometimes extreme, behaviour was unseemly. George Eliot, drawing on her own family history, famously bucked this trend and, in *Adam Bede*, painted an honest, accurate and quite charitable picture of Methodism at the close of the eighteenth century.[5] On the other hand, Arnold Bennett, the other novelist of Victorian Britain who comes to people's minds when Methodism in novels is mentioned, depicts Methodists, in novels such as *Anna of the Five Towns*, as "typical products of decaying Puritanism".[6] Anna's father's "holy valour for the pure doctrine" is matched only by his parsimony and unforgiving self-righteousness.[7] Of course, the self-critical character of the Victorian era, evident for instance in Charles Dickens's novels, serves as a supporting foundation for the better, reforming aspects of Methodism. Reflecting the steep decline in numbers and influence that the denomination has experienced since its heyday in the first decade of the twentieth century, which may or may not have had something to do with this austere reputation, Methodism makes less frequent appearances in British fiction in the twentieth and early twenty-first centuries. The concern of this book becomes, thus, to discover how Methodism has fared in these twentieth- and twenty-first-century novels. How accurate is its depiction in English fiction, and how strong is its presence in popular imagination?

Both to establish the focus of this study and to let the reader understand its author's assumptions, the three parts of this book's subtitle require introduction before the study gets under way: namely, Methodism, fiction, and the years since 1890.

Methodism: historical overview and denominational characteristics

In the family tree of Christian denominations, the place of Methodism among British churches survives now as uneasily as its hold in literature remains slippery. A cuckoo in the Christian nest, Methodism's origins are peculiar, its short history chequered, and its clearly-defined characteristics often, paradoxically, indistinct.

Founded almost unintentionally by the followers of John Wesley, who always wanted his converts to attend parish Communion, Methodism's roots lie in the Church of England from which it seceded soon after Wesley died. In 1784, Wesley, who had governed Methodists more or less single-handedly and quite autocratically throughout his evangelistic ministry, had made provision for their governance after his death. Under deed poll, he nominated one hundred people to be members of the "Yearly Conference of the People called Methodist" and indicated how their successors were to be appointed. This structure was to serve as Methodism's governing body after Wesley's death. Thus, soon after he died in 1791, Methodists found themselves, more by accident than by design, outside the established church, and, within four years, a "Plan of Pacification" was adopted by the Conference to allow for the administration of Baptism and Holy Communion in Methodist chapels. A declaration, in the same year, 1795, that the admission of a preacher to "full connexion with the Conference" conferred ministerial rights, effectively severed Methodism from its source. Methodists had evicted themselves from their parents' nest. So, unlike many nonconformist groups in Britain at the end of the eighteenth century who could trace their origins in a direct line to the Reformation, the Methodist Church's line of descent was by way of the Church of England.

As if proving the rule that the nature of Protestants is to protest and the nature of nonconformists is not to conform, nineteenth-century Methodism was riven with schism and secession, spreading in its various forms, according to the poet, George Crabbe, in his Preface to *The Borough*, like "spiritual influenza".[8] Even before the century began, the Methodist New Connexion split away in 1797 in protest at the concentration of power with ministers in the Conference. In 1805-6, discontents in the Warrington area formed an essentially lay movement, formally known as the Independent Methodists but sometimes nicknamed "Singing Quakers" because of Quaker elements in their structures. In 1807, Hugh Bourne and William Clowes organised the first Camp Meeting on Mow Cop in Staffordshire and, within five years, they had adopted the name Primitive Methodist because of their desire to return to a primitive, therefore presumably purer, form of Christianity modelled on the New Testament. Although Primitive Methodists, nicknamed "Ranters", were the most numerous, best-known and most long-lived of such splinter groups, other similar movements emerged in the early decades of the century, including Bible Christians (1815) and Tent Methodists (1820). The cracks continued to appear. In 1827, a dispute over the installation of an organ in Brunswick chapel resulted in a group of protestors in Leeds forming the Protestant Methodists; in 1832, the Arminian Methodists seceded at Derby over a point of doctrine, and, in 1842, Teetotal Methodists seceded in Cornwall. This ignoble history serves as illustration of the common tendency for groups to want to return to the most-pure source (which they always see as their position) and often behave most impurely in their efforts to get there.

In the early 1850s, the originating Methodist group, Wesleyan Methodists, was governed by an increasingly authoritarian Conference. Dissatisfaction with this led to a number of mass expulsions and secessions, most of whom joined forces in 1857 to create the United Methodist Free Churches and a minority of whom established the Wesleyan Reform Union in 1859. Others left and dissociated themselves from the Methodist movement entirely; the most famous of these was William Booth, first a Wesleyan then a New Connexion preacher, who left Methodism in 1861, eventually to set up the Salvation Army. As a result, by the end of the nineteenth century, the Methodist family of churches originating in the ministry of John Wesley was a diverse, but significant nonconformist group, alongside whom there were at least two other "Methodist" groups, one originating with George Whitefield—the Calvinist Methodists—and the other originating with Selina Hastings—the Countess of Huntingdon's Connexion.

Stevie Davies's forlorn comment in her novel, *Awakening,* that "factious Baptists pierce (Christ's) naked side with disputes as vicious as they are petty and self-righteous" could easily be equally appropriately applied to nineteenth-century Methodists. One of the two daughters of a Baptist pastor at the heart of this novel, Beatrice, imagines the robe of Christ torn to shreds by his followers as they drag their wounded Saviour this way and that between them.[9]

Sundered thus into many pieces in the hundred years immediately after Wesley's death, the ignoble story of schisms and secessions had shaped a complex Methodist family, open to being misunderstood but whose influence remained surprisingly strong. Towards the end of the nineteenth century, although the core group of Wesleyan Methodists enjoyed resurgence because it had built central halls in many large towns and cities which facilitated effective social ministry, the general direction of Methodism was towards reunification. This was fulfilled in 1932, when the main groups—the Wesleyans, the Primitives and the United Methodists with the inclusion of some smaller Methodist societies—united to form the British Methodist Church. Since then, however, in common with many other British churches, the denomination's influence on wider society in Britain has waned and its membership has decreased.

The particular course of the original formation and historical development of Methodism has forced it into carrying some anomalies. For much of its history, the Methodist Church thought of itself as a society, of which believers can choose to be members. The practice continues to this day in its dual assignation of its service welcoming adults into the church as "Confirmation and Reception into Membership", a duality reinforced in liturgical gesture and posture in that, at the moment of confirmation, the presiding minister first lays hands on the kneeling confirmand's head and then invites him or her to stand to shake his or her right hand. Annual membership tickets are also issued to the church's members. Many Methodists currently find this remnant of a bygone age awkward in that it sets up an uneasy distinction between outsider and those who belong, and sets more firm boundaries around the organisation than is customary in most churches. Furthermore, Methodists have never been Dissenters; rather, they are Nonconformists in that they have never been Reformed (in the sense of being party to the Reformation). But they are Protestant, and, following the style of John Wesley, they are both Catholic and Evangelical. Since 1932, the Methodist Church has been a broad church retaining, in its current liturgical expressions, both Wesleyan and Ranter elements. A Covenant with the Church of England, agreed in 2004, expresses its commitment to work more closely with the established church in Britain in acknowledgement of both Methodism's origins and its eventual destiny within Anglicanism.

In the contemporary church scene, when denominational loyalty matters less to churchgoers than shopping around to find a church whose worship style suits, the defining characteristics of Methodism are obscured. Its distinctive features include an almost unique form of church governance known as Connexionalism, which combines all local congregations under the authority of the annual Conference, presided over jointly by an ordained President and a lay Vice-President supported by a standing Methodist Council. The President, who serves for one year only, acts on behalf of the Conference when it is not in session. Doctrinally, Methodism is noted for its pragmatism; following the practices of Wesley, who exposed himself to criticism and hostility because he was sometimes prepared to set aside theological principles for the sake of the furtherance of Christianity, Methodism has been reluctant to resort to dogma and has left itself open to the charge of being unprincipled in its preparedness to accommodate new ways of thinking in its official statements. It has, for instance, been not far behind the vanguard on ethical matters, such as the marriage of people previously divorced, inter-faith dialogue and so on.

Social conscience, especially in the later years of the nineteenth, and the early years of the twentieth, centuries, has characterised many branches of Methodism. Methodists engaged themselves in the activities of the early Trades Unions, and Primitive Methodists were among the first leaders of the Labour Party. They sought to relieve poverty and unemployment with social programmes organised from the local chapel, and their campaigns against the hardships caused by the abuse of alcohol and gambling brought to the church a reputation for prudence, abstemiousness and "clean-living." Not always understood outside Methodism rests the fact that it also has a distinctive theology, often expressed in its hymnody (which is why Methodism is one of the few denominations in Britain officially to authorise hymn books for use in its churches). Mainstream Methodism has been Arminian in its theology[10] wedded to the belief that the Christian gospel is for all, that all can respond to it, and that no one is predisposed to reject it. Since Methodist union in 1932, the British Methodist Church has offered open hospitality at Holy Communion, in contradistinction with Methodism's original requirement to show a class ticket as proof of good standing in membership before admission to Holy Communion. The church has also emphasised an evangelical appeal to "all who desire to flee from the wrath to come"[11] and it has welcomed "sinners to the gospel feast."[12] This has often been expressed as the "Four alls", which Methodism's preachers are encouraged to learn and practise: all need to be saved, all may be saved, all may know they are saved and all may be saved to the uttermost. This led Wesley to an uncompromising commitment to Christian perfection and his followers to an equally uncompromising commitment to personal and social holiness. Every Methodist hymn book since the early *A Collection of Hymns for the Use of the People Called Methodists* in 1797 has, therefore, carried Charles Wesley's hymn "Let earth and heaven agree" with its neat summation of Arminianism, which Methodists trumpet as their distinctive rallying call:

> For all my Lord was crucified,
> for all, for all my Saviour died. [13]

In a similar vein, this minor English poet, but prolific and great hymn writer, enabled Methodists to sing in praise of "the Saviour of humankind" (originally, "the general Saviour of mankind") through whom God's "undistinguishing regard/was cast on Adam's helpless race",[14] and, in another hymn, Methodists respond with love to God's ...

> ...sovereign grace [which] to all extends,
> immense and unconfined;
> from age to age it never ends,
> enfolds all humankind. [15]

Other features of the denomination will be discussed in the course of this study, but this introduction to the movement contextualises twentieth- and twenty-first century novelists' depiction of it. Methodism did not live, move, and have its being in a vacuum, so consideration of the nature of the society in which novels depicting Methodists have been written and read becomes essential.

British society since 1890

The long nineteenth century ended and the twentieth century proper began on the outbreak of World War One, whose years of trauma had as profound and disturbing an effect on religious life in Britain as it had on European politics for the ensuing century. The highpoint of organised religious affiliation in England and Wales had been reached in 1905[16] and that of Wesleyan Methodism only slightly later in 1911.[17] Gradual, but inexorable, decline of formal religious observance, leading some to describe the century as the secular age, marked religious life in Britain from 1920. Indeed, the term "secular" has become convenient shorthand for the prevailing characteristic of British society since the Edwardian era. But describing modern Britain as secular is a matter of academic dispute. Questions arise. Are we secularised or secularising? Are we subject to the processes of secularism or secularisation? And what is the difference?

One problem in any religious discussion of the nature of contemporary society comes with awareness that secularism has several meanings. At its simplest, it can mean an attitude of indifference toward religion. It can also mean the systematic or programmatic process of disentangling religion from state or cultural powers, in other words the intentional weakening of religion both as an authority over our lives and an influence on how we think and behave. Furthermore, secularism can refer to the ideology that promotes this disentanglement. Usually this is a non-religious ideology, but, extraordinarily, secularising ideologues can be religiously motivated, as they were in nineteenth-century Britain when certain nonconformists argued for the formal separation of church and state.[18] Although the terms are often used interchangeably, readers will understand secularism to mean an intentional secularising programme and secularisation to mean an observable, if unintentional, process by which society has become inclined to observe religious practices. Whether or not British society is secularised or secularising depends on one's assessment of the completeness of the process.

Is British society secular? Strong indicators suggest it is. Not only have British churches lost the allegiance of about forty percent of the population over the course of the twentieth century, but sociologists of religion, such as S. J. D. Green, also identify trends through the century, including the growing acceptability of divorce, the drop in public esteem for the clerical profession, falling enrolments in Sunday Schools and a slipping away from Victorian ideals of Puritanism, as markers of secularisation. As long ago as the interwar years, Dean Inge offered the criticism that the "shakiness of church hierarchies" was accompanied by a rising demand for a more personal spirituality which had the deleterious effect of weakening our concept of the divine. When the successful transmission of religious belief from one generation to the next requires a measure of coercion, namely the subordination of the individual to the group, the demand for more personal spiritual autonomy and general distrust of authority militate against the survival of public religion.[19] British society has generally moved away from the habitual observance of public ritual and organised religion so that, by the early twenty-first century, unanchored spirituality floats free from institutions in Britain.[20] Charles Taylor famously dubbed this theory of secularisation "the subtraction story," a narrative in which religion constantly concedes ground to secularity, or in which, to use Green's vivid image, the abandoned country garden gradually merges into the surrounding wilderness. This process became a concern to early American Puritan preachers, and they used the image of the "wall" and the "garden." The wall around protected religious practice was always under attack, allowing the wilderness to invade and choke the garden. The role of the preachers became that of guardians of, and on, the wall to keep the garden safe. Indeed, A. W. Plumstead's book of collected Massachusetts Election sermons carries that title, *The Wall and the Garden*.

The other side of the coin, however, instructs that, as a whole, the world is more religious than it was and points to indicators that suggest religion is resisting secularisation in Britain. Any assertion that British society has moved away from religious observance must be qualified by the observation that religious beliefs, habits, and assumptions persist sufficiently strongly that, for instance, in the event of an accident or a tragedy, the public outpouring of grief includes informal, but no less compulsive, ritual such as the placing of flowers at the scene, as well as formal occasions such as organised observations of silence and well-attended memorial services, sometimes in cathedrals, but often in local churches. The persistence of such quasi-religious practices forms an incorrigible resistance to the flattening-out effect of secularisation. Evidence points to the innate religiosity of humanity that cannot help but reach out beyond itself into other dimensions and the realm of transcendence. The philosopher, Philip Kitcher, argues that the secular humanism, which he embraces, allows for the possibility, even the probability, that there is more to life than meets the eye.[21] He calls this secular humanism "soft atheism" as opposed to the dogmatic, so-called militant atheism unthinkingly covered in press reports. For him, the extra dimension of transcendence probably exists, yet modern humanity lives a secular life. Though most people in "western" society lead secular lives, they cannot help thinking theologically, behaving religiously, and feeling spiritual. According to Green, any secularising process in Britain had bottomed out by 1960, mainly as a result of non-Christian migration from Commonwealth countries being balanced by Christian migration from the West Indies, Africa, and Eastern Europe, as well as the development of new religious movements, but also because humanity simply and naturally refuses to live in the bleakness of secularity.

What's more, the assumption that religion was once stronger than it now is, which lies behind all suggestions that religion is weakening and non-religious understandings of life are gaining ground, should be interrogated. How religious was the working class at the time of the industrial revolution in Britain and how religiously observant was society at the dawn of the modern era? The story of the emergence of Methodism suggests that earlier populations were less observant of organised religious practices than is often supposed. The "good old days" were worse than imagined. Wesley and his first preachers travelled to where the need was greatest, where the church was often absent and where people were largely unchurched, a calling within them that resulted in urgent missionary zeal for America.

Of course, the question, problematised by the language used, creates difficulties. The binary distinction between religious and secular bequeaths instability. Take, for instance, one of the commonly suggested indicators of a secular society—the falling number of weddings conducted in churches. The Marriages and Civil Partnerships (Approved Premises) Regulations Act 2005, which came into force in the December of that year, liberalised the rules governing the conduct of weddings and permitted the licensing for weddings of venues other than churches and register offices. The Act was a statutory instrument laid before both Houses of Parliament on 15th November 2005, and the journals of both Houses show that no debate took place.[22] However, the clause forbidding the use of any religious content in weddings conducted in venues other than churches was commonly understood to have been included to preserve the interests of the Church. Since then, the contorted efforts taken to classify what constitutes a religious song, and even when a prayer is or is not a prayer, and all the resulting anomalies indicate the falsity of the sacred-secular division.

Full appreciation of these complex sociological and political arguments, based as they are on complex research and statistics, lies outside the scope of this brief introduction, whose purpose is merely to open our awareness to the potential of art to address the problems of secularity. Rowan Williams, former Archbishop of Canterbury, superbly placed to offer a view based on experience, offers the opinion that secularism reduces everything to functionalism.[23] He helpfully distinguishes between two forms of secularism. He calls one procedural, by which he means a public policy not to privilege one religion over another. This poses no problem to Christians. He calls the other form of secularism programmatic, meaning the process by which every public showing of religion is ironed out so that loyalty to the state enjoys supremacy over loyalty to religion. Such denigration of religious expression is, in his view, a problem both because it reduces moral decisions to the level of private choices and because it restricts individual capacity to criticise the state, whose rationality cannot be guaranteed.[24] However, because secularism does not give priority to the way God sees the world—Williams, of course, writes from a faith perspective—the secularising movement is doomed and cannot flourish. In contrast, art is necessarily un-secular, to use William's precise but unorthodox term, inasmuch as the arts host aesthetic and religious discourses.[25] Thus, the arts are capable of sustaining the imaginative life, and, in communicating both religious and irreligious themes, they continue to flourish in our contemporary world despite threats to their public funding. Novels are part of this art world and their publication continues to flourish.

Why fiction?

Novels with religious settings and spiritual themes—novels retelling biblical stories, novels fictionalising the stories of great Christians, novels set in religious communes, monasteries and churches, historical novels using religion and its practices to establish the context of the plot and novels whose main characters are people holding or wrestling with faith—are plentiful in recent decades, despite the current decline of organised religion and its public influence. The arts have replaced religion as the arena in which a secularised public may be permitted its continued exploration of theological and spiritual concerns. Because literature is written about what matters most, the essentially ultimate concerns of religion inevitably interest many novelists. Perhaps this explains the persistence of religious, theological, and spiritual themes in novels written in a nation and an age when organised religion is in decline. The novelist and critic, James Wood, is not alone in discovering fiction when he lost his faith, loving it for "its proximity to, and final difference from, religious texts" and seeing it as "the nearest thing to life."[26] Seemingly, even irreligious and atheist writers cannot resist the impulse to deal with theological matters.

The poet and critic of culture, Matthew Arnold (1822-1888), popularised a particular view of progression in enlightened inquiry, in which literature replaces religion as the means by which moral and spiritual values are conveyed to modern people; as religion declines in influence, literature becomes more powerful. This Arnoldian view and any of its variants depend upon the binary of religion and secularity. We may have relied too much on Arnold's theory, for the complexity of the religious scene at the beginning of the twenty-first century, where religious fundamentalism continues to spread despite postmodern suspicion of metanarrative, where religious progressives concerned about human rights and environmental justice emerge and speak out, and where there has been a so-called theological turn in philosophy and critical theory, means not that the modern self is necessarily secular, but that religious faith is expressed differently.[27] Religion has not disappeared; it has, rather, been displaced and relocated. For many, its expression, its ritual and its exploration arise in places other than churches, temples, synagogues and mosques, as if God's Spirit roams around to find an expression outlet denied in formal religious venues.

Religion and theology inhabit stories. The philosopher, Don Cupitt, remarked that stories have a dirty name:

> In common speech stories are very often untruths, tall stories, whoppers, self-indulgent fantasies, fictions produced by people who are romancing and have largely lost touch with reality. Stories are myths, fairy tales, just-so stories, old wives' tales, idle superstitions, or folktales told merely to terrorise the gullible. ... A typical story-teller is the salesman, seducer or

> con-artist whose line, spiel, story or patter is carefully designed to deceive. Novels, apocryphal tales and legends are bywords of untrustworthiness (his emphases removed).[28]

Yes, but stories are "make-believe"; they have the power to persuade and convince; they can bring hearers and readers into a different world, a different time and a different frame of mind. This power arouses some people's suspicion, and to this day, suspicion of the fiction-writer lingers in some religious circles. Within living memory, for instance, public scandal was caused in Britain when a radio play included ordinary dialogue for Jesus. Such attitudes exist despite a common belief that God inspires all human creativity, despite the concept of narrative theology which is evident in so many forms in the Bible, including the patriarchal narratives of Genesis, and despite the fictiveness of ostensibly non-fictional sections of the Bible. The biblical authors and editors used literary techniques, each of which introduced fictionalising elements, to explicate their theological, spiritual, ethical or religious purpose. The histories of the Old Testament are formally known as "the Former Prophets" in recognition that they are not objective history but theological or religiously nuanced narratives and the four Gospels of the New Testament are not biographies but proclamations of good news, propaganda in its non-pejorative sense. In common with all narrative, biblical narrative is inflected, and the presence of fictive elements within the Bible liberates it from a specific place and period to everywhere and all time. It acquires a make-believe quality.[29] This need not disturb any for whom the Bible's historicity is important; it did not disturb John Milton. Rather, Don Cupitt's use of the term "fictional theology" can have provocative and creative results. Theology is not fiction in the sense of "made up" (though it may be), but fiction conveys theology in that the story speaks to us of God and God's ways with the world.

Nevertheless, a crisis of confidence may have hit the contemporary story-teller. In his introduction to the modern novel, Jesse Matz wrote of the rise, in the latter half of the twentieth century, of metafiction–stories about stories, fiction about fiction and novels within novels–and he suggested that this self-conscious questioning of story-telling was caused by uncertainty about the power of fiction.[30] He dated this uncertainty to 1914, the year in which Henry James published an essay about the new novel, in which James worried about the future of fiction and its capacity to keep its sense of a "higher" purpose.[31] Matz argued that since then, whereas previous writers had been able to take a certain reality for granted, modern writers have had to be quite purposeful from the outset in asking "What is reality?" and "How can a full and authentic report of reality be given?"[32] In a century where scepticism has prevailed, and truth claims are tempered by relativism and irony, reality cannot be regarded as an absolute "transcendent, permanent, god-given certainty, but a matter of how you see it."[33] Nor can truth. Writers have presented their own view of reality and their own understanding of what is true. Consequently, in the present age, fiction that preaches is unacceptable. "Good" fiction shows without telling. Mimetic fiction, which is un-preachy and non-didactic, with its open endings, frayed edges and depiction of quotidian life, has unravelled plot but it has also given readers "the feel of immediate realities [with] new powers of precision, sensitivity and evocation."[34] In this sense, fiction has not lost any of its power as "make-believe." Indeed, these developments give readers greater power to delineate the meaning of the story—immensely theological in the sense of individual choice in life matters.

At least four significant features of story account for its persistent power and for its continued capacity to host religious, theological and spiritual exploration in a manner meaningful for those who seek this outside organised or institutional religion. First, stories form an essential part of who we are: "I am," said Cupitt, "the story I can tell about my own life."[35] These life stories will lack total coherence, they will have loose ends and they are likely to threaten to fall apart at several points, yet they are an indispensable aspect of our being. Moreover, they will not exclusively be about us; others' stories and a story of the Other will impinge on our story. Second, stories have the capacity to be open-ended. Real life holds more unanswered questions than there are full and final explanations and story-telling is valuable as a way to deal with the contingency of both unending stories and the presence of extraneous details.[36] Third, stories encourage curiosity in that when we listen to a story we embark on a search not only for what happened next but also for significance, and this can cultivate a wide-ranging and continuing search for understanding which will probably include at least some aspects of theology, the spiritual, or religious orientation. Fourth, stories share texts. Although reading appears to be an exercise carried out silently by an individual in isolation, shut away from distractions, reading is dialogue between writer and reader and conversation with other readers, other writers and other texts. Such communal texts can carry significance beyond that of the text itself; the story can carry ultimate and eternal significance. Fiction can, indeed, lead us to the Ultimate and the Eternal.

In short, human beings deal with their deepest spiritual, moral, and religious matters by telling stories, so, in a world of declining religious observance, novelists and artists have become surrogate priests, showing a world beyond what meets the eye, showing glimpses of a better place. For this reason, the important task of this book is to take notice and give an account of what novelists say about one of the world's religious expressions—the branch of Christianity known as Methodism. In a secular age, more people gain their perception of church second-hand, mediated or filtered by the novels they read, than through first-hand experience so *how* the Methodist Church is depicted in such novels should be noted.

In the chapters that form the main body of this book, different facets of Methodism will be examined. Chapter one begins this task by tracking how Methodism was previously depicted in literature. Its description of the literary legacy left by eighteenth- and nineteenth-century novels with Methodist themes and characters sets the historical and literary contexts for subsequent chapters. Chapter two discusses novels published in the first decade of the twentieth century. These show a marked change in the novelistic treatment of the denomination and the chapter includes appreciation of the transitional contribution of Arnold Bennett to the genre of Methodist novels. The novels discussed in the third chapter explore the Methodist denomination as a movement with political and social influence. Methodism's founder, John Wesley, called the world his parish, and his successors have had a social conscience which has had distinctive, and sometimes counter-cultural, expressions. The complexities of this facet of Methodism found expression in Howard Spring's *Fame is the Spur* and Sir Arthur Quiller-Couch's less well-known *Nicky-Nan, Reservist*. Chapter four considers the nature of Methodist faith, not the specifics of its beliefs, but the relationship between faith and doubt in some historical novels featuring Methodists. In common with many Christians, Methodists have wrestled with this faith-doubt tension. Many contemporary novels use the belief-disbelief antithesis as the dramatic focus and impulse for their plots, in the process making valuable contributions to the way readers understand and deal with one of modern life's most persistent conundrums. The chapter focuses specifically on the small number of recent novels that use Methodist contexts for their exploration of this tension. Chapter five concentrates on Methodist preachers and preaching featured in the novels discussed in the previous chapters. The significance of this chapter resides not only in the fact that Methodism is renowned for its preaching, but also for the role played by sermons in British literature generally. Throughout the story of literature in English—from Chaucer to Iris Murdoch—sermons have been embedded in fiction for all manner of reasons and, despite both the crisis in the pulpit in the contemporary church and the reduced exposure of the general British public to actual preaching, as well as the way preaching has been brought into disrepute by the haranguing of extremists, contemporary British novelists continue to feature preachers and their sermons in their books.[37] The fifth chapter also analyses the sermons encountered in the books discussed in previous chapters and asks what impression of Methodism they give their readers. The concluding sixth chapter draws this book's discussion to a conclusion.

As well as preaching, Methodists are also famed for their hymn singing. This reputation comes primarily from the contribution Charles Wesley and, to a lesser extent, his brother John made to Christian hymnody. Wherever hymns are sung in English, Wesley hymns feature prominently. Surely, every Christmas, wherever English is used, carollers sing "Hark! The herald angels sing". Inevitably, so important are Wesley hymns to the formation of Methodism that some are referred to in the novels discussed in subsequent chapters, but not frequently enough to allow them to form the basis of a chapter. Instead, as a sort of homage to Methodist hymns and Methodist hymn singing, each chapter uses a quotation from an appropriate Wesley hymn as its chapter title, as does the book: "Yet alive?"

CHAPTER ONE

OUR HIGH CALLING'S GLORIOUS HOPE

Widespread, but not universal, enthusiasm excited members of the several branches of Methodism when they convened in 1932 to unite as the British Methodist Church. Many of the groups that had seceded at disputatious moments in nineteenth-century Methodist history had found sufficient remaining common ground to bury differences. They could now reform as "the greatest Protestant church in the world" founded at "the greatest event since the Reformation" as some newspaper headlines shouted. This "greatest event" was the Uniting Conference of September 1932 held in the Royal Albert Hall attended by the future King George VI, then Duke of York. Formalities included the signing of the Deed of Union and celebrations included thousands of voices combining to sing Methodist hymns as well as the ancient *Te Deum*. At this Conference, an extraordinary version of an annual event, there was a strong sense of disparate branches of Methodism returning to the fold of the mother Wesleyan Church. Most saw it as a great opportunity for the Methodist church to address the challenge of a slow decline in membership. The three main strands of Methodism had already passed their peak. Wesleyan Methodism membership had peaked in 1911 and membership of the Primitives in 1908, whereas the United Methodists had never been as numerous as when they came together in 1907 (an omen Methodists chose to overlook when they united in 1932). More than twenty years of falling numbers had taken their toll on the strength of the movement.

In the year following the Uniting Conference, the popular novelist, Joseph Hocking, published *Not One In Ten*. Hocking was one of the most successful of a rash of Methodist novelists from 1880 on[1] and had published two dozen or more novels in a career spanning several decades. With his equally prolific brother, Silas, and sister, Salome, they had cornered a market for romantic Christian, specifically Methodist, fiction, which many readers relished as wholesome fare. Criticism within his own novels of more libertarian authors reveals Hocking's motivation; he wanted to provide Christian readers with a safe alternative to other fiction of his day, about which he expressed the opinion that it had an infinitely lower standard of morality than was prevalent in the fiction of twenty-five years previously.[2] Similarly, in America, many Methodists distrusted fiction because of its perceived pernicious effects on public morality, and a Methodist Episcopal Campaign against reading novels was run from 1865 to 1914 because novels were seen to be at the root of many social evils including urban crime, high divorce rates, mental illness and the general degeneration of the American character.[3] Even Thomas Jefferson said he would never allow his daughter to read a novel. The unanticipated result of this campaign was the rise of authors of Methodist background such as Stephen Crane and the now lesser-known Upton Sinclair, as well as non-Methodist authors choosing Methodist characters or settings for their novels. Among these was Harold Frederic's *The Damnation of Theron Ware*, the publication of which in 1896, somewhat disingenuously, sets the approximate starting point for this study. Although American by birth, Frederic spent many years in Britain and his novel was published here under his preferred title, *Illumination.* His British residency permits his novel to serve as a starting point for the study of how Methodism has been depicted by British authors in the long twentieth century. Its double, paradoxical title (how can a damnation be illuminating?), which was changed for reasons of publishing sensitivities, has been recognised as so significant that the book is now published with both titles. This paradox of illuminating damnation became a recurring theme in later novels where worthy Methodists descend into moral or spiritual depths and, in doing so, find their true selves; they lapse, or backslide, into darkness and find enlightenment. Hocking's Methodist characters often follow this trajectory, but, as Hocking was himself an ordained Methodist minister, no one should be surprised that his depiction of Methodism in the early years of the twentieth century is honest enough to include its faults and failings; he described it as he found it and experienced it. He expressed his disappointment with the Methodist Church when it failed to achieve its goals and he showed his admiration for its potential.

The main character in *Not One in Ten* is a young probationer minister, Robert Penhale, stationed in 1931 to the fictional town of Bedruthan where there are five separate Methodist chapels, an attractive squire's daughter, a notorious town drunkard, and a challenge awaiting him. He is better educated than many other Methodists of the time yet in his naïvety he dreams an impossible dream; he longs for the heart of Thirza Bedruthan, the soul of Zacky Krust and Methodist Union. Like most of Hocking's novels, this is a romantic comedy in which Penhale switches between dislike of Thirza for her headstrong priggishness and love of her as the queen of his heart and the light of his life (206). What unites Penhale, in his vocation to ministry, and Thirza, in her disregard for religion resulting from a liberal education, is a shared sense of despair about Christianity's purposelessness if it does not change people's lives for the better. Penhale grows despondent when he realises that not one in ten of the population can be found in church on Sundays, and his despondency is exacerbated by his colleagues in ministry, some of whom seem resignedly to accept that the 1930s are not church-going years, that the church is losing ground, and that the Methodist Church has been reduced from a working-class movement to a "respectable organisation" with well-educated ministers and well-off members (72). Penhale's enthusiasm for Methodist Union waxes and wanes throughout the novel, but this is mainly because he will support it only if it is something more than the rearrangement of chapels, an ecclesiastical game similar to that of moving the deckchairs before the Titanic sinks. He wants union to make the Methodist Church a more effective vehicle for change within people and society.

The novel's interest is in Penhale's relationships with other local clergymen, lay Methodists, the townsfolk, the gentry, and his own ideals (including what he thinks about church unity). Foolishly, Penhale stakes his vocation on Zacky Krust. He doubts whether his belief is strong enough to sustain his vocation to ministry, so he determines that if he has not converted the drunkard who has resisted all previous attempts at reform by the end of his first year in circuit, he will resign. Zacky's deteriorating behaviour at first manifests only in some heckling during the Bible reading in the first Christmas Day service that Penhale leads. But actions worsen into abuse, and threats directed towards one of the young women in the chapel and actual violence as he is evicted, all the effects of drink, dishearten Penhale. This, though, is a romantic comedy; after Methodist Union has been achieved and just before the end of Penhale's first year in circuit, Zacky comes to Christ. Religious revival hits Bedruthan and, although Penhale was initially rebuffed by Thirza and rudely rejected by Thirza's father when the young minister, who has turned several young women's heads, asked for Thirza's hand, there is still hope for the relationship at the end of the novel in that the headstrong Thirza challenges her father's assumption that she and Penhale are parted forever. His vocation and his love both seem intact.

The central impossible dream in *Not One in Ten* is the dream of Methodist Union after more than a century of schism. Five different Methodist churches exist in Bedruthan alone. On his first meeting with Thirza, who feigns interest in Methodist Union to engineer an opportunity to converse with the new minister, Penhale argues the case for union on the basis that there was

> a Wesleyan Church, a Bible Christian Church, a Primitive Methodist Church, a United Methodist Church and the Methodist New Connexion all

> in the same town. None of the Chapels was half filled, and as far as I know the difference between them was the difference between Tweedledum and Tweedledee. It is true the Bible Christian Church, together with the Methodist New Connexion and the United Methodist, arranged for some sort of Union a few years ago, but I am afraid as far as Bedruthan was concerned it was not a great success (20).

Hocking, always an intrusive narrator keen not to demand too much of his readers, later calls this unsuccessful union in Bedruthan "a paper Union" (72). In chapter twenty-three of the novel, Penhale joins local Methodists on an excursion to London to attend the Uniting Conference. Hocking's fictionalised account of the event captures the excitement of the occasion. Although Penhale expresses some disappointment at the lack of spontaneity and passion in the Conference's formal pageantry, he nevertheless knows it has been a wonderful day and hopes that those present were "alive to [its] real inwardness" (244), which sadly does not find visible expression in Bedruthan.

This optimistic depiction of what Hocking unashamedly insists on calling "the greatest Church in the world" (298) builds on a literary tradition in which Methodism had variously been the butt of satire, attracted stringent criticism, aroused suspicion as a dangerous popular movement and, in some instances, received a sympathetic reading. This literary tradition, formed of well-known novelists and their work in the eighteenth and nineteenth centuries, comprised the background against which twentieth-century novelists wrote.

In a review of a late nineteenth-century study of Methodism in the literature of the previous century, C. T. Winchester commented that it should cause little surprise that few eighteenth-century writers gave any attention to Methodism because "the truth is the polite literature of the eighteenth century and the Methodism of the eighteenth century appealed to quite different classes."[4] Literature was for the drawing room and the club, whilst Wesley's and Whitefield's work was for the labourer and the lower middle class whom Winchester reckoned poets, dramatists and essayists largely ignored. Even so, authors who did give their attention to Methodism offered interesting critiques of the movement. These include Richard Graves and Tobias Smollett, each of whom published lively satires of Methodists in successive years.

Graves's *The Spiritual Quixote, or the Summer's Ramble of Mr Geoffry Wildgoose* was the only novel the Rector of Claverton published throughout a prolific writing career in which he wrote vast quantities of now forgotten prose. In 1752, Graves had been piqued when an itinerant preacher had visited his village and emptied the parish church of worshippers. After evicting the unlicensed preacher, Graves determined to write a satire on Methodism. He began to write it in 1757 and published the novel in 1773, by which time his grievance against Methodists had reduced in intensity and he may have been beginning to see some merit in the movement. The novel's "Quixote", Wildgoose, is a young squire, recently returned from Oxford, who is fond of mixing with villagers, especially with a half-witted cobbler named Jeremiah Tugwell, who becomes his Sancho Panza. He had already fallen out with the argumentative parish priest over whether a door can be called a window in the context of the Window Tax, so there was little hope of future cooperation with him. The example of outdoor preachers who visit the village inspires Wildgoose to venture out as an itinerant preacher, especially after discovering some old sermons on a dusty, high shelf among the furniture he inherited with his mansion-house. In his sermons, he confesses enormous quantities of imaginary sins and, after delivering them, he quenches his thirst with ale from the Manor cellars. His friend, Tugwell, imitates Wildgoose and repeats his arguments. Soon the squire decides to tour the country with Tugwell and preach like the Methodists. The remainder of the novel, picaresque in its style, continues their adventures in which Wildgoose emerges as a powerful preacher whose fame spreads far and wide. The usual pattern of his sermons was to begin by lamenting the general corruption of humankind, in the process threatening his hearers with the terror of hell. He would then offer a tender description of God's mercy before using a range of metaphors, which he varied to suit his audiences, to show the way to salvation; to the lewd, he spoke of nuptials, to the thirsty he spoke of streams and feasts, and to the covetous he spoke of hidden treasures. Generally, the success of his preaching was short-lived (73-5). Nevertheless, when he is introduced to George Whitefield, the latter is envious of Wildgoose's evangelistic success. Many have shown that Graves is far from original when plotting the novel: he includes variations of events taken from Smollett and Fielding and he transfers to his novel many incidents reported in John Wesley's *Journal*. Clarence Tracy's annotated edition of the novel identifies several cross-references such as the account of religious frenzy in the Captain Johnson episode of the novel (294) which replicates the entry for 11th August 1740 in Wesley's Journal.

Despite Graves's criticisms of Methodists for self-righteousness, for neglect of humbler duties in order to spend time in prayer and for arousing mass hysteria, the author nevertheless appears to admire some Methodist qualities and frequently expresses disapproval of individual Church of England clergy. He makes fun of innkeepers who lock up their valuables when they know Methodists are about and, after one landlord has expressed disapproval of "Methodites or Mithridates" for being so profane as to sing in such a house as his (140), Graves has him change his tone and admit, on the basis of hearsay as he has never attended any Methodist meetings, that they are nevertheless "a good sort of people" who "did a great deal of good in the world, and were very charitable to the poor, and they preaches main well" (142).

Wildgoose's peregrinations as an itinerant preacher come to an end when he receives a slight head wound. He had been attempting to preach at Warwick races and was knocked on the head with a decanter in a brief fracas. The shock was greater than the wound and he was sent to bed for a day. This brings him to his senses and he returns to his Mother Church. Later Wildgoose meets Dr. Greville who is portrayed so sympathetically that Graves seems to be presenting him as an ideal parson who recognises both the abuses in the Church of England and the contribution Methodism has made in awakening "indolent and careless Christians" to these failings.

> [He] really was what Mr. Wesley and his associates ought to have been, and what (I sincerely believe) they at first intended to be. He revived the practice of primitive piety in his own person, and in his own parish; and, by his examples and admonitions, excited many of the neighbouring Clergy to be more vigilant in the discharge of their duty. He had a faith, which worked by love; or, in modern language, his belief of the truths of the Gospel made him consider as an indispensable duty those acts of beneficence which his humanity prompted him to perform (432).

This affirmation of Wesley's intentions tempers the novel's satire to such an extent that critics, such as T. B. Shepherd,[5] have sometimes asked whether *The Spiritual Quixote* is Graves's own vicarious venturing forth from the confines of the Church of England. Reputedly, the author rarely left the village of Claverton in fifty years. Perhaps he longed for the open road. Wildgoose, a free spirit whose behaviour is difficult to curb, on the whole behaves foolishly, but he retains readers' sympathies to the end. Dr. Greville, actually and figuratively, walks Wildgoose home in the final scenes of the novel, bringing his adventures to an end on the estate he will soon inherit. *The Spiritual Quixote*'s satire, although begun in anger, actually gives as little offence as a gentle ramble on a summer's day.

Only two years earlier, in 1771, the first appearance of a Methodist as a prominent character in a British novel had occurred in Tobias Smollett's *The Expedition of Humphrey Clinker*, published in the year the author died. Smollett had, until this late stage in his life, lacked sympathy for the Methodist movement, having written a bitter attack on its imposture and fanaticism in 1764. Carrying the assumption that his antagonism continued into the final pages he wrote has proven to be an easy mistake to make, for closer examination of the novel reveals that in the intervening years he must have continued to investigate the movement with an open mind and his views had ameliorated by the time he wrote *Humphrey Clinker*. The eponymous Methodist, Clinker, is a simple fellow, but he is neither a clichéd hypocrite nor a small-minded puritan. He introduces himself to his employer as one who can

> read and write and do the business of the stable indifferent well—I can dress a horse, and shoe him, and bleed him, and rowel him; ... and then I can make hog's puddings and hob nails, mend kettles and tin saucepans. ... I know something of single-stick, and psalmody, I can play upon the Jew's harp, sing Black-ey'd Susan, Arthur-o-Bradley and divers other songs; I can dance a Welsh jig and Nancy Dawson; wrestle a fall with any lad of my inches, when I'm in heart ... and I can find a hare when your honour wants a bit of game (29).

Later in the novel, after Bramble has reprimanded Clinker for haranguing a crowd, Clinker explains that he had been preaching a sermon arguing against swearing to a group of poor people. Bramble begins to respond that this class can never be cured of their ills, but Clinker insists that, if they can be made aware that what the preacher has in mind is nothing but their wellbeing and their improvement, they will listen patiently and be convinced. When Bramble exasperatedly remarks that there would then be nothing to distinguish them from their betters, it is clear that the target of Smollett's satire is not the Methodist but the one who argues against him (199). When Tabitha Bramble and her servant pretend to join the Methodists, she gives the impression that she is much happier than ever before. Again, this supports the suggestion that Smollett had dug beneath the stereotypical portrait of the Methodist as a long-faced puritan; he had recognised their happy anticipation of the joys of heaven and observed smiling faces among their number.

Humphrey Clinker's intertwined narratives of the Bramble family and their servants paint a complex picture of Methodism. On the one hand, Tabitha uses it as a dating agency, and her servant expresses trust in the Lord but hedges her bets by sewing witch elm into the hem of her petticoats. On the other hand, Clinker cannot resist preaching to his fellow prisoners when he is mistakenly gaoled on a charge of highway robbery, and the movement is generally seen to benefit human society. In short, Smollett's is what Anderson calls "a soft and kind" portrait of Methodism;[6] he admires his unimpeachably pure creature, Clinker, and represents Methodism with the fairness that follows a more than superficial understanding of its beliefs and practices. Shepherd avers that Smollett's final novel is "as much an apologia for Methodism as it is a criticism."[7]

The same cannot be said of Henry Fielding and Laurence Sterne, both of whom expressed their antagonism towards the upstart movement. Fielding's *Joseph Andrews* and *Shamela* do not, of course, restrict their biting satire to Methodism; the novels offer a broad satirical snapshot of religious practice in England at the beginning of the evangelical revival associated with George Whitefield as well as the Wesley brothers, and the author's criticism extends to an exposé of Church of England malpractice.

In *Joseph Andrews*, much of the criticism levelled against the revivalists is doctrinal. That which concerns Parson Adams is not Whitefield's criticism of wealthy clergymen and the corruption of Church power, for, as a poor curate, Adams knows that abuse of power and wealth has impoverished many. He is more concerned that Whitefield has "set[...] up the detestable Doctrine of Faith against good Works" (70), thereby lessening the imperative for Christians to be charitable to their neighbours. Fielding cites several instances to illustrate that preoccupation. In one, Parson Trulliber professes to believe all the Church's doctrines and to have faith, yet he refuses to help Adams in his time of need and, in another, the author informs readers that Shamela's library includes two of Whitefield's recent and popular publications but "with only the Duty to one's Neighbour torn out" (332), as Shamela has been assured that her profession of faith and regular church attendance are sufficient in themselves. Adams carries concern also for the related matter of "enthusiasm", by which is meant not only zealous behaviour but also the belief that God reveals God's self to individuals directly without the mediation of the Church and its duly licensed officers. Adams, like many others, saw danger in this; if anyone can claim to speak for God, many could be led astray.

Parson Adams's concerns about, and criticism of, Methodists are no worse than any expressed by many actual churchmen of the day, but examination of Fielding's Methodist characters reveals a deeper authorial antipathy towards the movement. In *Tom Jones*, Jones and his companion, Partridge, go to the Bell Inn in Gloucester. The hostelry is highly recommended by Fielding because it has escaped all Methodistical taints. The landlord of the inn is Whitefield's brother who is, however,

> absolutely untainted with the pernicious principles of Methodism, or of any other heretical sect. ... His wife is at present as free from any Methodistical notions as her husband; I say at present; for she freely confesses that her

> brother's documents made at first some impression upon her, and that she had put herself to the expense of a long hood, in order to attend the extraordinary emotions of the Spirit; but having found, during an experiment of three weeks, no emotions, she says, worth a farthing, she very wisely laid by her hood, and abandoned the sect (vol. 1, 327).

Fielding's gratuitous assault on Methodism here dismisses it as a pernicious heresy, a sect and a fraudulent movement duping potential followers into false expectations. Worse insults aimed at the integrity of the movement follow. At the end of the novel, once Tom Jones has married, Fielding settles in Blifil in the north of England where "[h]e has lately turned Methodist, in hopes of marrying a very rich widow of that sect, whose estate lies in that part of the kingdom" (vol 2, 411); in other words, Fielding questions outright the purity of the motives of those who join the movement.

In other Fielding novels, Methodists fare little better. In *Miss Lucy in Town*, Mrs Haycock explains to Lord Bawble that the prostitute Jenny is not dead but "worse, if possible—she is—she is turned Methodist, and married to one of the brethren" and this is no good thing (14). In *Amelia*, a grave-looking man named Cooper approaches Booth in prison and engages him in conversation. Cooper suggests that Booth should not despair that he is in prison because, whatever his crime might have been, his imprisonment might be the means by which he is called to conversion. Fielding comments that Cooper "ran on for some considerable time with this cant, without waiting for an answer, and ended in declaring himself a Methodist" (155). That Fielding calls his evangelism "cant" and that it is persistent and without respect for the hearer seems to be sufficient criticism in itself. Fielding, however, reports that Booth later finds his pockets empty. The only possible culprit is Cooper. When Booth offers a reward for the return of his snuffbox, Cooper quickly brings it back, claiming to have found it. To Fielding, Methodists are much worse than dangerous heretics peddling through their unrelenting preaching a twisted doctrine of salvation; they are hypocrites and rogues.

Other writers of the time, Horace Walpole, Samuel Johnson, Alexander Pope and Thomas Chatterton, were equally dismissive of Methodists. These contribute to a discernible general anti-Methodist air in eighteenth-century literature, but, as none of them wrote novels, they fall outside the scope of this brief survey of the ground on which later novelists built.

Laurence Sterne, another vehement critic of Methodism, does merit consideration. His innovative, anarchic works cross conventional literary boundaries and blur the distinction between fiction and fact. His sermons, whilst many were actually preached from his pulpit, trespass into the world of fiction in that they were published as the sermons of his fictional character, Parson Yorick, a persona through whose name Sterne refers back to "a fellow of infinite jest, of most excellent fancy", the deceased friend of Shakespeare's Hamlet.[8] Playful, cross-generic writing such as Sterne's is often fecund, for the capacity to read texts within and across different genres adds depth of meaning. Indeed, the sermon on The Abuses of Conscience Considered that Sterne uses in *Tristram Shandy* has a dual existence; it was first written and preached to a congregation in York Minster in 1750, then subsequently incorporated into the novel which he completed in 1767. That the sermon was well-received by readers of the novel prompted Sterne to rush into publication two volumes of sermons he attributed to the fictional Yorick. His preface to the volumes includes an explanation, the level of seriousness of which is difficult to ascertain. Was Sterne's tongue firmly in his cheek when he wrote these words?

> I suppose it is needless to inform the publick, that the reason of printing these sermons, arise altogether from the favourable reception, which the sermon given as a sample of them in Tristram Shandy, met with from the world; – That sermon was printed by itself some years ago, but could find neither purchasers nor readers, so that I apprehended little hazard from a promise I made upon its republication, "That if the sermon was liked, these should also be at the world's service;" which, to be as good as my word, they here are, and I pray to GOD, they may do it the service I wish. ... as the sermons turn chiefly upon philanthropy, and those kindred virtues to it, upon which hang all the law and the prophets, I trust they will no less be felt, or worse received, for the evidence they bear, of proceeding more from the heart than the head.[9]

In the long run, it is a matter of judgement whether anti-Methodist sermons, of which there are four in the collection, can be counted as philanthropic or, indeed, whether they can be of service to the world, but Sterne believed them to be so. The four in question are Sermon XIV on Self-Examination, Sermon XXV on Humility, Sermon XXXVII on Penances and Sermon XXXVIII on Enthusiasm.

Fifty years ago, Arthur Cash's discussion of the sermon in *Tristram Shandy* pointed out that part of Sterne's thesis was that, because self-knowledge is available to people when it is diligently sought and accurate self-judgement is equally available, no one can seek excuse for moral faults on the grounds of ignorance.[10] Sermon XIV, whose text is Isaiah 1:3 in which the people of Israel are chastised for not knowing their God whereas even the ox and the ass know their masters, addresses this problem. Sterne, in his fictional persona of Yorick, argues that a giddy, thoughtless and intemperate spirit is common among the human race, and that people must be naturally inclined to address and correct their faults, otherwise they will not see them. He uses Jesus's parable of the Pharisee and the publican to highlight five ways people go wrong when examining themselves before God. In a manner which becomes typical of Sterne's preaching, he presents himself as steering a middle course, looking to one flank to fault Roman Catholics and looking to the other flank to fault Methodists and other enthusiasts. In this sermon, the preacher levels a charge against Catholics and identifies the fourth error as that of entrusting to others the work of self-examination by asking priests to identify and address personal faults, whilst the fifth error is one revived by Methodists, that of attempting to prove individual good works by the degree of indulgence in spiritual enthusiasm. Sterne takes up this point again in sermon XXV on Humility, where he alleges that Methodists are as full of extravagant conceit as Quakers are in their readiness to claim that the Holy Spirit has descended upon their silent meetings. He expresses his view that it is difficult to argue with spiritual frenzy and wishes there were more cool heads and sound judgement among his contemporary Christians. He claims that it is equally difficult to argue with someone whose riposte is "We feel it is so." In this sermon, he seeks meekness and lowliness of heart modelled on the life, character, and ministry of Christ. He despairs that, within Methodism, there are some serious and deluded members and that the sect is a "disordered body" (471). In sermon XXXVII, Sterne self-identifies as the moderate Christian once again. He says that God does not intend people to be in sackcloth and ashes, so Sterne is critical of Methodists who descant upon the need to alienate themselves from the world and sell all they have. He ascribes this self-denial to misplaced enthusiasm, misplaced because God makes provision for human happiness (520). The next sermon on Enthusiasm (XXXVIII) prolongs the criticism of Methodists for their self-conscious manifestations of extreme spiritual behaviour, which the preacher believes demonstrates a lack of trustful dependency on God. In contradistinction with this showy and emotional Methodist behaviour, Sterne asserts that Christianity is "the most rational, sober, and consistent institution that could have been given" to the human race (528). He prays that we may, at all times, see that this is so.

Cash's concluding assessment of these sermons is that "[a]ll of the [sermons'] scattered attacks on Methodism, Romanism and enthusiasm in general ... are intended as rebukes of blind, unreasoned faith, which to Sterne is always pernicious."[11] For Sterne, the duty of religion was to have the fear of God before the believer's eyes, yet he wrote in the liberal spirit which allowed humankind to approach the divine with dignity and self-respect.[12]

Taking these four writers together, Graves, Smollett, Fielding and Sterne, common ground in their response to Methodism can be seen; each of them was, to some extent, suspicious of its emphasis on the individual before God, not only in the way individuals felt able to claim a call to preach, then preach without licence, but also in the individualistically subjective manifestations of spiritual enthusiasm. The threat of indiscipline and lack of control resulting from these features cast fear into the hearts of these writers who hoped the movement would soon fizzle out like many another fashionable craze. However, Graves and Smollett were much more lenient in their judgement than Fielding and Sterne, and showed in their novels that Methodism brought enlightenment and opportunity to many simple and uneducated people. By the end of the eighteenth century, most commentators saw that, because of the rise of Methodism, the Church in England would never be the same again, and, early in the nineteenth century, most writers accepted the merits of Methodism more readily. Indeed, throughout the nineteenth century, novels with Methodist influences, themes or characters were in general more sympathetic to the movement than their predecessors had been. The Establishment felt less threatened by Methodism as it settled into denominational status and functioned less as a radical movement and more as an evangelical church.

In the middle years of the nineteenth century, the great Methodist novelists were George Eliot and the Brontë sisters, with whom no later novelists using Methodist characters or exploring Methodist themes could fail to be familiar. Charlotte, Emily and Anne were all born before their father, Patrick, was appointed as incumbent in Haworth, a parish with a surprising number of Methodist associations, but Haworth was where they spent their formative years and lived out their lives. John and Charles Wesley, John Newton and George Whitefield had all preached there, the latter in the presence of Selina, Countess of Huntingdon, on which occasion, by amazing coincidence, two men in the congregation had dropped dead. For over twenty years, from 1742 to 1763, William Grimshaw, whom Wesley admired so much he designated him as the likely successor to himself and his brother, was rector of Haworth parish.[13] Wesley had been impressed by all that had been achieved there. The Brontë sisters' mother, Maria, was Methodist and, although she died quite soon after their move to Haworth, her husband remained pro-Methodist and was full of what Valentine Cunningham calls Methodist tales and impressions. Patrick Brontë, for instance, refused to hang curtains at the rectory windows, lest the family had to escape a conflagration similar to that from which the young John Wesley fled in his father's Epworth rectory. Charlotte inherited her mother's copy of Wesley's abridgment of the *Imitation of Christ.* Two Methodist influences on the family more permanent than Maria, who died when the girls were still young, were their aunt, Elizabeth Branwell, a Methodist from Cornwall, and their long-serving servant, Tabitha Aykroyd, who was a class leader at the Wesleyan Chapel, who remembered Grimshaw and who served the household until she died at the age of eighty-five. In later life, Patrick attended West Lane Wesleyan Chapel for Sunday evening worship. This combination of Anglican practices, Methodist influence and participation in some Methodist activities strikes children of the twentieth century as unusual, but was far from unusual in some deeply religious households of the nineteenth century.

Given that history, Methodism had a profound influence on the Haworth parsonage household and on the novels the sisters wrote. [14] The precision of Charlotte's use of Methodism comes as no surprise. In chapter nine of *Shirley*, for instance, she tells of the congregation at Briar Chapel jauntily singing a range of hymns to a variety of tunes, always passing from one to the next with ease. Charlotte displays an accurate knowledge of Wesley's Methodist hymnal, *Collection of Hymns, for the Use of the People Called Methodist*, extracting from it a number of hymns from several sections of the book, including an extract from Wesley's Birthday Hymn. She replicated the words perfectly well, but it can be inferred from the few inaccuracies in the way she sets out the hymns, for instance, setting out a stanza of "Oh who can explain" as eight lines of five syllables whereas in the original they are printed as four lines of ten syllables each, that she knew the hymns by heart and, working from memory, set them out wrongly.

Emily, though precise in the structuring of *Wuthering Heights*, its complex time frame, its multiple narratives and the intricate genealogy of the household, shows much less precision than her older sister in her depiction of religion. The distinction between Church and Chapel when defining Joseph's religion in *Wuthering Heights* seems to matter little to her and, at the end of the novel, any readers trying to identify his church affiliation are still in the dark. In chapter thirty, he goes to chapel with Zillah; Mrs. Dean explains that he goes to the kirk but she is unable to say whether this is the Methodists' or Baptists' place; he expresses predestinarian views in chapter nine, which are not in keeping with Methodism; and, later, Mrs. Dean says he might be a Baptist after all. Unlike Charlotte, for whom religious detail in her novels is important, Emily is content with this imprecision. Nevertheless, Cunningham argues that Emily allowed her "Methodistical" upbringing to serve in her novels in two ways, firstly as a referent for passion and, secondly, in its provision of a rhetoric for passion.[15] With regard to the first function, Emily used Methodism as a shorthand referent for extremes of feeling, behaviour and religious enthusiasm. In chapter seventeen of *Wuthering Heights*, Heathcliff locks himself in his room and, grief-stricken, wails and moans *in extremis*. Emily conveys this to her readers quite simply; she says he was "praying like a Methodist" crying out to his father as much as to God (180). With regard to the second, Catherine's avowal to Nelly that "If all else perished, and [Heathcliff] remained, I should still continue to be ..." (84) serves as an example of rhetoric borrowed from Wesley's hymns to serve as declarations of love between characters.[16]

Three essays in a collection discussing the literary art of the youngest Brontë sister, Anne, identify three distinct features of her art that are indebted to Methodism: life writing, witnessing, and the play of emotions on the religious life. First, Melody Kemp uses what she calls the original sense of Methodism as an "ordering of one's time" (195) to argue that Anne was inspired in her narrative technique by John Wesley's endorsement of self-examination through the use of journals, his own being an outstanding example. Kemp sees the centuries-old tradition of journal writing, beginning with life writing such as Augustine's *Confessions*, as a method by which their subjects strive towards the perfection of holiness by analysing their flaws and resolving to make improvements. She sees this practice, in *The Tenant of Wildfell Hall*, in both Helen Graham's diary and Gilbert Markham's epistolary self-representation and suggests that both Helen and Graham are impelled by a Methodist imperative of self-improvement through self-examination (197). Not at all unique to Methodism, spiritual autobiographies, confessions and conversion narratives also featured in Puritan practice where journal keeping replaced the priest's function in the assurance of salvation for Catholics. Wesley, too, saw the spiritual value of journals. Second, early Methodism progressed through various forms of witnessing, most especially in open-air preaching, in which personal testimony was often present, as well as in regular class meetings in which Methodists were required to give account of all that God had done for, and within them, since they last met. Deborah Morse notes that Anne Brontë developed multiple forms of witnessing in her novels to achieve several of her aims, which included a radical critique of male dominance, the advancement of women's education and the enhancement of women's role in society. She also uses a form of witnessing to shape, within the novel, a vision for the future in which the role of women in society has been enhanced both by their education and enfranchisement as well as by the diminution of men's dominance and violence. Third, Lee Talley discovers that all the Brontë sisters plundered 1798 to 1812 editions of the *Methodist Magazine* owned by the Haworth Parsonage family from which they could rework received notions of gender in their stories. Anne, she suggests, also developed her critique of society, as expressed in *The Tenant of Wildfell Hall* from these Methodist sources.[17] Anne's first novel, *Agnes Grey*, had displayed similar Methodist traits, most notably in the narrator's insistence in probing the emotional and psychological factors in the story of her past using the language of the heart that shares its rhetoric with Methodist doctrine and practices.[18] Too much store should not be given to this interest in psychology, emotions, and feelings; most novels were moving in this direction.

Nevertheless, few can doubt the influence of Methodism on the Brontë sisters and few can fail to detect Methodist traits in their novels. Their work was soon followed by a greater Methodist novel, George Eliot's *Adam Bede*.

Many read *Adam Bede* as the archetypal Methodist fiction. Geoffrey Parrinder acclaimed it as "the great Methodist novel,"[19] neither because of its piety nor because it functions as a denominational tract, but because it carefully and sympathetically depicts the hymns, prayers and preaching of the movement. This care and sympathy result from the complexity of Eliot's own religiosity. Having been brought up in an evangelical Anglican home, the young Mary Ann Evans was devout. She held prayer meetings at school, practised acts of self-denial and argued for predestination with her aunt. However, at the age twenty-two, she swung to the opposite end of the religious spectrum and refused to attend church. She had already proved to be a scholar and was engaged to translate some important theological works, namely Strauss's *Life of Jesus* which involved early scholarly criticism of the New Testament Gospels, Feuerbach's *Essence of Christianity* and Spinoza's *Tractatus* and *Ethics*. Some of this scholarly work caused her to reassess her own religious stance; she did, indeed, in a letter to a friend, outline three stages in her religious development from the "strong hold that Evangelical Christianity" had on her early years, through an antagonistic attitude that led her to renounce "*any* belief" to her mature lack of "antagonism towards any faith in which human sorrow and human longing for purity have expressed themselves; on the contrary, I have a sympathy with it that predominates over all argumentative tendencies."[20] This mature position enabled Eliot, now well-known by this pseudonym, to write accurately, honestly and charitably of Methodism in *Adam Bede*, of Jews in her last novel, *Daniel*

Deronda, and of evangelical Anglicans in her first fiction, *Scenes of Clerical Life*.

Eliot used three main characters in her historical novel, *Adam Bede*, and a host of occasional references by other minor characters, to construct a picture of the theory and practice of Methodism in the rural England of 1799. The chief representatives of Methodism in *Adam Bede* are Seth Bede, Dinah Morris and the Reverend Irwine. The novel opens as Seth and his brother Adam are at work as carpenters. Workshop banter reveals Seth to be an absent-minded Methodist who makes a door but forgets to add the panels. Detractors allege that Seth is over-preoccupied with religion to be of any earthly use, but Adam, who is not a Methodist, charitably speaks out in his defence, intimating that Methodism has turned many an idle fellow into an industrious one. At the very least, Methodism does no one any harm.

Dinah Morris is soon introduced; she is preaching in a field just outside Hayslope. She is not what the villagers had expected. Neither ecstatic nor bilious, she is quiet and respectable in appearance and demeanour. She preaches in a clear voice and is not overexcited in manner. Rather, she lovingly and gently beseeches her hearers to personal repentance. In a paper appraising Eliot's depiction of Methodist in *Adam Bede*,[21] James McConnell demonstrates that Dinah's message is very similar in style to actual Methodist preachers of the time, such as Mary Bosanquet Fletcher, whom Dinah cites in the novel when she is asked whether women's preaching is allowed in the Methodist society (87). Mrs Fletcher was not Eliot's model for Dinah Morris. Rather, Dinah is loosely based on Eliot's aunt Elizabeth Evans. The sermon so closely follows Wesley's pattern that it is small wonder that readers have assumed that Eliot copied one of her aunt's actual sermons.[22] Moreover, Dinah's visit of Hetty in prison is reminiscent of an occasion in Eliot's aunt's ministry when she visited an imprisoned child murderer who was refusing to confess. Eliot's aunt prayed with the prisoner through the night until she confessed then accompanied her in the cart to the place of execution.[23] Dinah, like Eliot's aunt, is nothing other than sincere in her calling to preach and nothing other than meticulous in practising what she preaches. In a note of historical accuracy, Dinah's permission to preach is withdrawn at the end of the novel by the sixtieth annual Methodist Conference of 1803, when the Wesleyan Church changed its mind on women preachers on the dual basis that many members disapproved of women preaching and that there was no shortage of male preachers. To compensate and console women preachers who did not want to be silenced, if any woman felt compelled in a calling to preach, the Conference allowed her to address her own sex and those only.[24] At this point in Methodist history, Elizabeth Evans left the Wesleyans, unlike the fictional Dinah who remained with them. For the sake of literary accuracy, caution should be used when identifying Dinah with Eliot's Aunt Elizabeth. In her journal account of the composition of *Adam Bede* in November 1858, Eliot strongly denied the identification, saying,

> The character of Adam, and one or two incidents connected with him were suggested by my Father's early life; but Adam is not my father any more than Dinah is my aunt. Indeed there is not a single portrait in 'Adam Bede'; only the suggestion of experience wrought up into new combinations.[25]

The distinction Eliot made is that she did not use actual people as models for her characters; she drew on their experiences to form fictional characters. Dinah emerges from the novel as an outstanding representative of early Methodism, so much so that she is referenced in Leslie Church's history of early Methodist people, almost as an historical figure.[26]

The Rector of Hayslope, Reverend Irwine, is the third character to mediate to readers the nature of Methodism in *Adam Bede*. Unlike most of the villagers, Irwine perceives neither Dinah nor the Methodist faith as a threat to the dignity of the Anglican Church. He assumes, first, that the preaching will not become a regular occurrence and, second, he reminds the villagers that Methodism had already transformed a wild, drunken wife-beater into a man who is thrifty and decent. He considers interviewing Dinah about her preaching and permitting a frank and supportive exchange of views that he felt would assist the Methodist movement. Thus Irwine shows himself to be far more laissez-faire about the incursion of Methodism into his parish than any previous fictional parson had been.

Adam Bede bears the marks of an historically grounded understanding of Methodist belief and practice and provides an accurate and honest portrait of Methodism at the close of the eighteenth century, from the vantage point of a further fifty years of experience of the movement in which Methodism had grown into acceptability. Unlike the eighteenth-century novelists who discussed Methodism, Eliot, looking back on the eighteenth century from the nineteenth, is neither over-critical of, nor over-sentimental about, the movement, although her praise for it is not without qualification. Eliot's portrait of Methodism is as positive as anyone could hope for, far from hypocritical and not in the least prosaic.[27]

If these are some of the novels that gave readers at the close of the nineteenth century their impression of Methodism, what defining characteristics of Methodism do they identify? From reading of Methodists in these noteworthy novels, would readers consider Wesley's followers a good influence on society? Or would they fear Methodism as a dangerously unruly, charismatic and individualistic sect? Firm answers to these questions are difficult to offer. From Smollett and Graves, readers would find plenty about Methodism and attitudes towards it to mock, if they took Fielding's and Sterne's criticisms to heart they would regard Methodism as a dangerously extremist form of Christianity, and if they accepted the portrait depicted by the Brontës and George Eliot they would regard it as beneficial for both the individual soul and the cohesion of British society. That there was no common mind among eighteenth- and nineteenth-century novelists on the subject of Methodism may be no surprise, but it is important to note that the variety of views about Methodism in earlier literary incarnations paves the way for its similarly inconsistent reception by twentieth- and twenty-first-century readers. A four-square building cannot be erected on an uneven foundation.

CHAPTER TWO

THE MILLENNIAL YEAR RUSHES ON TO OUR VIEW

At the beginning of the twentieth century, Methodism took severe literary body blows from the work of Arnold Bennett who revived the tradition of novels dismissive of Methodists as members of a distasteful or hypocritical sect whose zealous, and sometimes extreme, behaviour was unseemly. He depicted Methodists as "typical products of decaying Puritanism,"[1] in novels such as *Anna of the Five Towns* where Anna's father's "holy valour for the pure doctrine" [2] is matched only by his parsimony and unforgiving self-righteousness. Bennett's hatred of Methodism was deep. He hailed from the Potteries where the Methodist Church had a strong controlling influence over the working population. He saw it as the religion of traders and artisans which effectively reinforced the status quo and restricted aspiration. Other religious commentators were more generous towards the movement; they saw it as a force for good, keeping the working population from slipping into destitution. In Bennett's novels, Methodism cannot deliver and heal people, though it is part of their everyday life. It captivates and restrains them. For instance, it cannot deliver Anna from the control of her miserly father or prevent his merciless cruelty towards her and others—he drives a tenant who owes rent to suicide. Bennett believed that the ecstasy and emotional excesses of early Methodism had been elided from the religious expression of later generations so few, if any, of his characters take joy in their religion. They are gloomy, forbidding, sober and sombre people as a result of their religious practice and beliefs. In *Clayhanger*, a preacher at a Methodist rally remarks that "even for the veriest little infant on a lorry, there is no escape from the eternal fires save by a complete immersion in the blood" and, in *These Twain*, when Auntie Hamps dies, prayers take place in the house before the solemn funeral procession to the church. Notably, "in the house she had been paragon of all excellence—in the church, packed securely and neatly in her coffin, she was a sinner snatched from the consequences of sin by a divine sacrifice." Indeed, Bennett had depicted her as saint and sinner; she was an important and influential member of the church and a generous giver, but she had also been a vicious and cruel mistress to her servants. Bennett's recurring theme stresses that what is said and done in church on Sunday is not carried over into actions on Monday; the hour or more in church serves as a time of self-delusion and illusion. This rather damning novelistic portrayal of Methodism among third or fourth generation Methodists corresponds with Bennett's personal views seen in the (possibly apocryphal) story of Bennett and a companion walking past a Methodist chapel in London with a poster inviting passersby to "Prepare to meet thy God." In response to the words on the poster, Bennett forlornly remarked, "Why do they never say, Love thy neighbour?" According to a prominent Methodist literary critic of the time, Dorothea Price Hughes, whose husband was President of the Wesleyan Methodist Church in 1898, Bennett showed "the noxiousness of Methodism."[3]

The phenomenon of dichotomous readings of British Methodism as simultaneously beneficent and malign can be demonstrated in Theron Ware, the protagonist of Harold Frederic's *The Damnation of Theron Ware* or *Illumination*. Frederic's story of a man's journey from certain faith to confused doubt, conducted always within the scope of his ministry in the American Methodist Church until, ultimately, he resigns the ministry and heads for Seattle with Alice, can be read as a fall or an awakening, or as both. Even so, Methodism is not always liberating in the novel: Alice Ware, for instance, finds that it isolates, rather than frees her, to the extent that she despairs that God may have forgotten her. Indeed, none of the novel's characters, several of whom doubt God's existence, finds God.[4] At the time Frederic was writing, American Methodism was being torn apart by conflict between liberals, who held an optimistic belief in the inevitability of progress, and conservatives, who balked at the modernising trends of liberals, and Frederic places this conflict at the heart of his novel. Theron Ware's problems begin when his attempt to introduce modern ideas to the Methodist congregation in his new appointment in Octavius is rejected, and he seeks solace elsewhere—in Celia Madden's paganism, in Father Forbes's Catholicism and in Sister Soulsby's pragmatism.[5] Ware's inability to assimilate modern religious views and integrate them into his church scuppers him. Although Frederic employs some of the conventions of sentimental religious novels of his day, and Theron Ware undergoes two or three conversions, these are always subverted. The novel has no conventional happy ending; rather, Theron Ware's illumination becomes a return to his mundane existence unchanged in every respect except for questioning the existence of God. Of course, as

Father Forbes tells Ware, the modern church must always compromise, and a believer's faith and future are always ambiguous.[6]

Bennett and Frederic form a literary transition from the nineteenth into the twentieth century, as far as the fictional depiction of Methodism is concerned. Their realist novels depict the way modernist thought challenged the Methodist Church in Britain; it could either try to adjust or be pushed into an anachronistic backwater. Once the twentieth century had dawned, Methodists, along with everyone else, were faced with rapid changes in society. Conventional religious assumptions faced severe challenges. Industrialisation enjoyed advancement with all its accompanying inequities, traditional forms of government received challenges from both evolutionary and revolutionary democratisation processes, fresh scientific insights troubled some of the certainties of traditional religious thought, and the new technologies of war affected large numbers of non-combatants. Life and its currents changed forever. Could old-time religion respond? How would literary Methodism fare among these major concerns? Would Methodism stand its ground in twentieth-century novels? Two novels published in the first decade of last century do not bode well for the future of Methodism in literature; they hark back to the Methodism of old and set their narratives, in the case of one, to the time of the Wesleys and, in the case of the other, to the chaotic period soon after their deaths.

The first, *Hetty Wesley* (1903), is one of a series of thirty Tales and Romances written by Arthur Quiller-Couch, a Cornish writer best known for his editorship of poetry anthologies for school children for Oxford University Press, used until well into the third quarter of the twentieth century. His unfinished autobiography, published posthumously as *Memories and Opinions of Q*,[7] reveals that Quiller-Couch, who was so well-known that he used the single letter pseudonym Q, had an unusually nonconformist religious background for an establishment figure. Although he was a confirmed Anglican, he was familiar with Methodist ways. Considered to be "stiff in Methodist ancestry," his family lived opposite the Wesleyan manse and, for a while, his father nursed the very ill Wesleyan minister, although by then Quiller-Couch's father had married and had become Anglican. The autobiography supplies a child's eye perspective on a nonconformist service he attended with an evangelical grandparent. Musicians in the gallery led the singing and the worship leader, Pastor Hine, had a fine voice for reading the lesson, but it flattened to a droning, soporific monotone when reading his forty-minute-long sermon (37). The bookcase in his grandparents' home stocked nothing but sermons and clergy biographies, the limited choice of reading similar to that Jeanette Winterson, many years later, famously complained about in her religiously-repressive foster home. As with Winterson, Quiller-Couch's literary future was unimpeded by such restricted reading matter. However, he found much of the preaching he was submitted to, with the anodyne exception of Pastor Hine's, much more disturbing. The young Arthur was so terrorised by hellfire preaching that he listed two "maturer religious beliefs" (40) he declared himself unlikely to revise. One was his belief that it was both stupid and wicked to terrorise a child with a fear of Hell, for one should not make a child fearful of God, and the other was a belief in the essential goodness of humanity which is strong enough to resist and outlive the effects of any cruelty in the Church's doctrines or actions. The Church might burn heretics and pronounce the souls of unbaptized infants damned, but neither action nor declaration can kill the essential goodness of humankind. This optimistic belief in humanity fuelled Quiller-Couch's novel-writing.

Hetty Wesley fictionalises the life story of Mehetabel Wesley, the most educated of Samuel and Susannah's six daughters. A second edition of the novel, published five years after the first, included a preface in which Quiller-Couch expressed both delight that the novel had been well-received by the reading public and satisfaction at its literary reception, for critics had been kind to a book in which Quiller-Couch himself knew there were deficiencies. He had, however, been thoroughly disappointed that "leaders of Wesleyan thought" had condemned the book as a caricature of the Wesley family. His preface defends his novel against this onslaught by asserting that the novel is a "plain marshalling of facts" drawn from documentary evidence. In researching the novel, he consulted actual correspondence among the Wesley family and, whatever his Methodist critics feel about his portrait of Samuel Wesley, they cannot deny that it is derived from actual historical evidence. Twenty years later, Quiller-Couch reported that criticism had died down in the face of demonstrable fact. His defence against his Methodist critics draws attention to the hybrid nature of *Hetty Wesley*. Published as a novel, it masquerades as a biography by using footnotes and actual correspondence between members of the Wesley family. All except one of the letters in the novel are original, and the invented one, reasonably, fills a gap in a chain of correspondence between Hetty and her father and uses Hetty's reply to give the tenor and content of what Samuel had written to her. The novel also includes poetry, *A Mother's Address to Her Dying Infant*, actually written by Hetty Wesley after her third child was stillborn (232) and, later in the novel, another of her poems, purportedly found on a tear-stained sheet of paper, demonstrates how far down towards the depths of sorrow Hetty travels, while still battling bravely to find encouragement and support by "clutch[ing] at the weak roots of love" (242). To attempt a fictionalisation of the Wesley story was, perhaps, bound to court controversy among, and criticism from, Wesleyans, but Quiller-Couch's obfuscation of the boundary between fact and fiction in this genre-busting work, postmodern before its time, is unusual in its intentionality and clarity of signposting. All life-writing blurs this border.

In four parts, with an additional Conclusion and Epilogue, *Hetty Wesley* explores themes of forgiveness, the nature of vows and the tensions associated with the desire to be faithful. Although set primarily in Lincolnshire in the Wesley household whilst the children, including John and Charles, are young adults, the novel also visits India and London, as Susannah seeks news of her brother who has recently returned from Bombay on an East India Company trading ship, *The Albemarle*, and as their descendent, General Wellesley, campaigning in the Berar mountains, discovers an abandoned hermit's cave. Indeed, the novel begins and ends in India and opens with the mystery of the sudden disappearance of Susannah's brother on docking in London from overseas. The mystery is pushed to the background and never fully explained, so that the stronger element of the novel tells the tragic story of Hetty's several thwarted relationships and the depiction of Methodism's "first family." Quiller-Couch effectively uses the story of Hetty's life within, and on the margins of, a troubled family, first to explain why Methodists were later regarded as people to trust. More specifically, the writer seeks an explanation for why the Duke of Wellington would always prefer to be leading a band of Methodists than men of any other persuasion. Quiller-Couch also plumbs the depths of the tensions that exist both when individuals are torn between love for one and loyalty to another and when families are racked between the desire for forgiveness and the expectation of obedience.

In a strikingly pertinent example of Biblical typology, Hetty tells the children in her Bible class the story of Joseph. They recognise a good story and are held wrapt in the tale even though they could easily have been distracted by snow sliding from the roof of the schoolroom. One of the children interrupts the class and, seeking clarification, asks whether Joseph is the oldest of Jacob's twelve sons. At first, the boy merely expresses his perturbation that Joseph was such a braggart, but then he asks the question many in the Wesley household must have dared not ask: "Miss Wesley—you're not a boy, of course—but how would *you* feel if your father made everything of one of your brothers?" (89). Hetty, like Joseph, is one of many children: six daughters—Emilia, Molly (baptised as Mary), Hetty, Nancy (formally Anne), Patty (registered as Martha) and Kezzie (christened Kezia). Hetty Wesley has a more troubled life than some of her sisters, each of whom might have suffered as a result of the unfeeling actions of their unsympathetic father, made worse in Hetty's case because he disapproved of her independent mind and wilful behaviour. Samuel, rector of Epworth, tyrannises the Wesley household with his choleric bad temper and rash misjudgements often expressed as vows which he believes he is thereafter bound to keep. For instance, he forbids any of Hetty's sisters to attend her wedding to William Wright. Of the girls only Molly, a handicapped child, is capable of standing up to her father. Pointing a finger in her father's grey face, she protests on Hetty's behalf:

> You are a tyrant to those you love: and now in your tyranny you are going to do what even in your tyranny you have never done before—a downright wickedness. Thwarted abroad, you have drunk of power at home till you have come to persuade yourself that our souls are yours. They are not. You may condemn Hetty to misery as you have driven—yes, driven—her to sin: but her soul is not yours and this secret of hers is mine not yours! (169).

Molly's father never forgot these words; he had no answer to them; he never again spoke a harsh word to Molly. What she had said was true. Earlier, Hetty had fallen in love with a local boy, Johnny Whitelamb, and the novel's narrator strongly implies that she was pregnant by him, but that she lost the baby. She ran away to Lincoln to marry him, but he had done nothing about obtaining a licence, so she was left alone and distressed. Angry, believing that Hetty had brought shame on his family, and disappointed because he had educated Hetty himself but now she had become a "wanton" (144), Samuel Wesley dismissed her from his home. Samuel, who had also played his part in bringing shame on the family in that he had served time in a debtors' prison shortly after John was born in 1703, was, however, still a bad debtor. He owed money to a plumber whose son, William Wright, travelled to Epworth to declare his love for Hetty and ask her hand in marriage, unaware that Hetty had already sworn to herself that she would marry the next man who asked her. Seeing this as his way out of financial trouble, Samuel agreed to the marriage and paid off his debt to the plumber. To her credit, Hetty chose to take what she believed to be the noble course, saying to William in the presence of her father:

> If, as I think, those who marry without love sin against God and themselves, my father is driving out sin by sin. I cannot love you: but what I do under force I will do with an honest wish to please. ... I will try to think it noble—to thank you for it all my days—to be a good wife (171-2).

The marriage proves to be disastrous. She gives birth to three children, none of whom live longer than a week. William Wright becomes a drunken abuser; yet, in blindly obedient loyalty when he is ill, "still [Hetty sits] beside him, her body aching, her heart cold, and watched him, hour after hour" (255). These are pathetic scenes. That Samuel Wesley's refusal to forgive brought Hetty to this condition cannot be denied. Her family loyalty had been tested when she had fallen in love with Johnny early in the novel, and she had turned to the Bible. Although her conscience dictated that she did wrong to meet her lover secretly, her religious training and the Bible gave her guidance with which she felt uncomfortable:

> When a mother has failed, even the Bible may fail. Hetty read her Bible: but just because its austere teaching had been bound too harshly upon her at home, she turned by instinct to the gentler side which reveals Christ's loving-kindness, His pity, His indulgence (87-8).

She craved to be good; she longed for forgiveness; she wondered why Christ could forgive Mary Magdalene yet she could not feel that he had forgiven her (162). She acknowledged that her road to forgiveness would be long but she was prepared to wait, for she still desired it. Ultimately, she wrote to her father pleading to be forgiven. The plea, as the reader expects, is denied, her father refusing to acknowledge any part in her troubles, even claiming in a letter (as actually written by the real Samuel Wesley) that matrimony, rather than causing her any harm, had in fact given her a good name (236).

John, or Jackie as the family calls him, who is absent through most of these events as he prepares for ordination, but whose ministry is the main reason why interest in the family exists, is the favoured Jacob of the family, emerging unsullied by most of the events. However, when he returns to Epworth, he preaches in a neighbouring church in Wroote. His sermon excoriates his father's behaviour and publicises the family's internal conflicts. He preaches on the text, "If you forgive others their trespasses, your heavenly Father will also forgive you" and alludes to the psalmist's belief that God will not despise "the sacrifice of a broken and contrite heart." He then declares that Christ, who drew a distinction between sin and the sinner, promised forgiveness for those who confess their sins, before concluding:

> With sorrow I admit before you that in the household to which you should reasonably look for example and guidance, ["a broken and contrite heart"] has been despised. What then? Are we wiser than Christ, or more absolute? (195).

Nothing more is said about this sermon, yet the question with which it ends is the question at the heart of this novel. Members of Methodism's first family in *Hetty Wesley* wrestle with the tension between loving forgiveness and the ideals of absolute observance of rules and adherence to vows. This makes them an interesting study. In Quiller-Couch's novel, the Wesleys are far from being a "collection of plaster saints" (vii).

Particularly daring for the turn of the century, the novel depicts one of the holiest characters in the book as Hindu. In the Prologue to Book III of the novel, this holy man offers food and hospitality to two hopelessly lost Britons serving the East India Company, one of whom is Susannah Wesley's brother. The hermit then guides them for two days to the interim safety of a rest-house where travellers will soon pass and lead them back to Surat. They want to repay him with a gift of money, but he firmly declines. They observe that he has not eaten throughout the journey, and the hermit says he will not eat for a further two days for a vow binds him to drink only from the spring near the hermitage and to eat only food washed in its water. When this is dismissed as madness, the holy man explains that a vow is binding; "a man makes [a vow] to his own hurt, perhaps, or to the hurt of another, or it may even be quite foolishly; but thereby he stablishes his life" (118). How does such a binding vow differ from the vows Samuel expected his family to obey? Is Samuel "madder" than the hermit? Why is the hermit's vow worthy of the readers' praise while Samuel's vows are not? The discrepancy does not exist because one religion is inferior to the other, but, rather, because the obligation to love one's neighbour has not been subjugated to the need to obey rules. Hardship has not been inflicted on a third party by adhering to the vow. The Hindu holy man is sanctified by his actions; Samuel's confessed holiness is compromised by his deeds.

Another Methodist novel published soon after *Hetty Wesley*, Sheila Kaye-Smith's *The Tramping Methodist*, a romantic thriller published in 1908, provides another example of the tension between religious ideals and the compromises so often necessitated by daily life. Set in a tumultuous Methodist era, eight years after John Wesley's death in 1789 and while Methodism was in process of seceding from the Church of England, the novel uses a quotation from Robert Louis Stevenson's *The Vagabond* as its epigraph:

> Bed in the bush with stars to see,
> Bread I dip in the river—
> There's the life for a man like me,
> There's the life for ever,

but its central theme is "love without sacrifice is dead" (265). As the wife of an Anglican curate who converted with her husband to Roman Catholicism in the 1930s, Kaye-Smith, herself, knew something of the cost of love. Her novel concerns, first, the adventures in love of Humphrey Lyte, whose amour, Ruth Shotover, is already betrothed to a man who leads a double life. Later, Humphrey's adventures extend when falsely accused and imprisoned for a murder whose perpetrator he believes he should protect. In the first chapter of the novel, Humphrey, the fifteen-year-old son of a clergyman, has a religious experience that instils in him a desire to lead a good life and a yearning for Holy Communion (6). From vague religious ideas, in childhood, of hell associated with an ill-kept church, he soars in vision to the house not made with hands (8) and becomes the eponymous tramping Methodist. Initially, he walks from town to village in search of a church with Holy Communion but, after falling into a swollen stream and recuperating with an hospitable Methodist family, he is soon travelling the roads of south east England preaching in the open air.

Kaye-Smith sympathetically foregrounds several characteristics of early Methodists. They are well-educated. As a young boy, Humphrey presents as an ill-read outdoor type. As time progresses, his conversion derives from his reading of Thomas à Kempis's *Imitation of Christ.* While he recovers from his fall into the stream, he acquires from the daughter of his hosts, Mary Winde, a young girl of his own age, a love of books. While staying with them he devours the writings of Spenser, Shakespeare and Chaucer so that he, like Wesley himself, becomes an avid reader. His religious awakening equates with a literary awakening. Nevertheless, the Methodists in the book show little evidence of their wide reading and choose to lard their rhetoric and conversation with the more limited language of the Bible. For a while, Humphrey accompanies the most experienced Methodist preacher in the vicinity, John Palehouse, who, like the other preachers, always prefers Biblical phraseology, choosing, for instance, to call preaching "prophesying". Scripture saturates his mind and nature (109-110) to such an extent that readers learn he rarely picks up a copy of the Bible to read as he relies on the fact that he knew it by heart. In the way that musicians, who play music by heart without going back to the score, know that they move increasingly further away from the composer's original intentions, so lack of reference to the text of the Bible poses danger, and, in the case of Palehouse, raises for the reader the important question of how far men like him stray from biblical authority. Kaye-Smith portrays this as a feature of restless courage. Despite being warned by the curate of Biddenden that Palehouse and Humphrey with their "demned ranting" are not welcome in the parish (133), they will not be silenced. They preach on the common, and before long an angry crowd jeers and hisses at them. The curate speaks to some rough-looking men on the edge of the throng, and the mob begins to hurl stones at them. Soon after Palehouse falls unconscious to the ground, the squire and three of his grooms intervene. Experiences like this deter neither Humphrey nor Palehouse; they have "an ever-increasing desire to resume [their] wanderings" (147).

Humphrey's father's earlier violent reaction to his conversion to Methodism, beating him before ejecting him from the family home (34), may have unwittingly prepared him for the difficult life of an itinerant preacher. If Kaye-Smith depicts Methodists in this era as courageous autodidacts with restless zeal, she also alerts readers to their faults. At High Halden, the local minister criticises Palehouse's "Puritanical" fanaticism, Humphrey's "Papist" longing for Communion and their "too free and easy" preaching methods (132). Here Humphrey encounters, for the first time, signs of decay and disease in the Methodist system; the more organised Methodism became, the more prone to decay it became.

Nonetheless, heroes exist among Methodists. Humphrey falls foul of a man called Enchmarch, the betrothed of his love interest, Ruth Shotover. Enchmarch, quick to belittle Humphrey and send him away (91), provided the reason, at a human level, why Humphrey was content to tramp the countryside with Palehouse preaching from village to village. In a later encounter, Palehouse recognises the supposed Squire Enchmarsh of Kitchenhour as none other than his scoundrel cousin, Harold Macaulay, who had already caused the downfall of young women. Humphrey believes he must rescue Ruth, but he cannot because illness has weakened him. Palehouse confronts Macaulay who defends himself from Palehouse's revelation and accusation by killing him. Humphrey witnesses these events in Plurenden Quarry and manages to obtain a signed confession from Macaulay who lets Ruth go in exchange. Arrested later for Palehouse's murder, Humphrey chooses not to hand in Macaulay although he possesses the written confession, but goes to prison himself to honour his agreement. Above all else, Humphrey is an honourable man. Readers understand that *The Tramping Methodist*, as a romantic thriller, will resolve all in the end to allow the tramping Methodist to marry his Ruth.

Kaye-Smith sets the narrative of her novel against a naturalistic backdrop. When Humphrey has fully recuperated after his fall into the stream, Nature rejoices, too; "The birds were singing gaily, and as we passed under the trees, so beautiful in their spring green, a robin began to trill and twitter" (65). By this and other similar references to Nature, the author pushes into the readers' consciousness the cosmos above, the weather, flora and fauna around, and the ground beneath, the ever-present settings of Humphrey's story. Nature's continual presence belittles the events and renders the life of this tramping Methodist small and inconsequential against the vastness of space and the wonder of Nature. Yet, because fiction readily hosts inconsistency, another possible effect is the opposite, aggrandisement of his life by making it part of the natural world. Humphrey lives his life in step with God's natural world, the implication being that Humphrey's life is part of the natural order and an integral aspect of the cosmos. That, however, does not overlook the fact that responding to his sense of calling as a preacher permanently damaged relations with his family, exposed him to danger and, at times, such as the period of his imprisonment, made his life intolerable.

As the new century dawned, to what extent does the literature of its first years see Methodists as forward-looking avant-gardes responding readily to the new challenges of the twentieth century? Had the Methodist movement left behind its noxious past? For much of the previous century, Wesleyan Methodists counted off the years by holding well-attended Watchnight Services at each New Year's Eve. The hymn from which this chapter's title is taken was sung at most of them. As a new century approached, Wesleyans looked forward to the twentieth century with great enthusiasm and, in 1898, launched a Twentieth Century Fund, more often referred to as the Million Guinea Fund, the aim of which was to raise a million guineas from a million Methodists for the building of central halls in British cities. It achieved its aim, thus facilitating important city centre mission and ministry in many major cities, much of which continues into the twenty-first century. None of this excitement translates to novels of the same era, in which Methodists are simply depicted as certain in their faith and zealous in their actions. At times, they are uncompromising. At other times, they are backward-looking. In both Quiller-Couch's and Kaye-Smith's novels, Methodism shows its decay; as it became more institutionalised as a church rather than a movement, novelists depicted it as slipping away from its original ideals. If these novels were written primarily for Methodist readers, a reasonable assumption, because Methodists, as the Hocking siblings knew well enough, were sufficiently numerous to form a sizeable market. In that case, Quiller-Couch reintroduced a note of reality and humanity that had been lost in the hagiographies of the Wesley story, and Kaye-Smith encouraged contemporary Methodists with Humphrey Lyte's derring-do antics, but with limited overall effect. The first decade of the twentieth century was the heyday of Methodism, yet its novelists prophetically cautioned

Methodist readers that they had slipped away from something important about Methodist aims and ideals. As the twentieth century began, they asked their Methodist readers to remove their rose-tinted spectacles and look honestly at what the prospects might be for a movement whose origins were in the eighteenth century and whose attitudes were still fixed in that era.

CHAPTER THREE

ON MERCY'S WINGS I SWIFTLY FLY

Of all of Charles Wesley's over six thousand hymns, "Jesus, the Gift Divine I Know," from which the chapter title comes, expresses most powerfully the Methodist impulse to preach and live a social gospel. Omitted from the most recent 2011 British Methodist hymnal, *Singing the Faith*, the hymn seeks for its singers the living water of God's Spirit. After they drink that water, they will thirst no more for finite happiness; rather, they shall enjoy peace and joy that shall forever stay and none can take away. Although the singer seeks this grace for himself or herself, others benefit. The presence of the Spirit within the singer is evident in the ensuing commitment to work for the relief of the needy:

> Thy mind throughout my life be shown
> While listening to the wretch's cry
> The widow's and the orphan's groan
> On mercy's wings I swiftly fly
> The poor and helpless to relieve
> My life, my all, for them to give.

The hymn concludes epigrammatically, a perfect example of how Methodists learnt their creed:

> The truth of my religion prove
> By perfect purity and love.

Such concern for the poor and needy as proof of religion's worth does not appear uniquely in Methodism, but that commitment occurs as a defining characteristic of the denomination in the first centuries of its existence. Among commentators external to Methodism who expected to observe social concern amongst Methodists was the nineteenth-century Congregationalist preacher, R. W. Dale, who said that the Methodist doctrine of Christian perfection should make them social reformers. Many were, but some were not. John Wesley himself was a curious mixture of conservative and reformer. As a reformer, his concern for the poor becomes evident in his preaching and his writing. His first open air sermon took Luke 4:16 as its text, and he declared throughout his ministry a love for the poor and a sense that they possessed a purer and more serious grace than the rich whose lives were mixed with paint, folly and affectation.[1] Above all else, he felt called to preach to the poor, but, as a conservative, he made no mention of the harsh poor laws of the time nor spoke against the barbarity of capital punishment for minor offences, to which the poor easily fell prey. According to Gordon Wakefield, Wesley had a romantic picture of poverty and took little or no political action to alleviate the hardships poor people endured. Indeed, the class meetings he encouraged all Methodists to attend may have fostered a culture of introspection which diverted their members' attention away from the need to improve the social conditions under which so many poor people lived. They may have encouraged acceptance of a bad lot and may have smothered the growth of a working-class consciousness. Elie Halevy's thesis, revived in 1957 by the Marxist historian Eric Hobsbawm, that the Methodist movement saved Britain from the rash of revolutions that spread across Europe between 1789 and 1848, depends on the theory that Methodism predisposed its followers to political apathy, a concept widely peddled among contemporary Methodists, but it does not entirely stand up to serious examination. Without question, Wesley would not have stomached among his followers any talk of causing political upheaval in Britain, but other factors also mitigate against English revolution. In England, the faster speed of industrial progress providing more employment for displaced agricultural labourers in Britain than in France, the stability of parliamentary government, and the controlling effect of the Justice of the Peace system were more important factors than the growth of Methodism in Britain's avoidance of the major problems that led to revolution elsewhere. Those who want to talk up Methodism and its historical role are still tempted by the theory, and, indeed, Howard Spring, one of the novelists discussed in this chapter, alluded to it in *Fame is the Spur* (490), but it exaggerates the influence of the denomination on wider British society.

Officially, both the Wesleyan and Primitive Methodist Churches discouraged their preachers from involvement in political action and did not allow church property to be used for either trade union or political meetings, but, in practice, many early Methodists were Socialists who involved themselves in working class protest. Records show that as early as the first and second decades of the nineteenth century, Methodists participated in the agricultural trade unions of East Anglia, Wesleyans were involved in the radical Trade Union Brotherhood in South Shields and, in Suffolk, Norfolk and Lincolnshire, chapels were frequently used for union meetings. Methodist union leaders numbered 486.[2] Methodism served as a school for public speaking and development of organisational skills among the working classes. In Methodist circuits of thirty or forty chapels with only one or two ministers (which was not unusual), the bulk of preaching fell to ordinary working men and women whose only primary education had been in Sunday School. Trained in the skill of argument and debate in chapel committees, circuit meetings, and business sessions, they had learned the art of governance and the management of financial matters if they held office as chapel stewards. They were well-equipped to work in the trades unions. Many unions mimicked the three-tiered Methodist structural pattern of national Conference, regional circuit, and local chapel; many also imitated the Methodist weekly subscription system to support the cause. In addition, many local union branches were called chapels. Methodism provided numerous Trades Union leaders. Six of the seven Tolpuddle Martyrs sentenced to transportation for life in 1834 were Wesleyan Methodists; Tommy Hepburn, the first leader of a mineworkers' union in Durham in 1832, was a Primitive Methodist preacher; Ned Cowey was the first president of the Yorkshire Mineworker's Federation; Joseph Arch, the founder of the National Agricultural Labourer's Union was also a local preacher on the Primitive Methodist circuit; and many more union leaders came from Methodist ranks. Eric Hobsbawm wrote of Primitive Methodist as "a sect of trade union cadres."[3] Later in the nineteenth century, Methodists became more overtly associated with Socialism, with prominent ministers such as Hugh Price Hughes (1847-1902) at the West London Mission declaring in 1884 that the great need of his time was for Christian Socialism and founding the "Forward Movement" which called Methodists of all its sections to social and political action. By the early decades of the twentieth century, a significant number of influential Labour politicians in local and national government were rooted in the Methodist Church, although, as might be expected, not all Methodists with an interest in politics had joined the Labour Party; many were Liberals and a few had other political affiliations.

Methodist commitment to social action and participation in party politics features in at least two novels of the twentieth century, Arthur Quiller-Couch's *Nicky-Nan, Reservist* published in 1915 and Howard Spring's better-known *Fame is the Spur*. Quiller-Couch's *Nicky-Nan, Reservist*, which the author called his heat-of-the-moment topical novel to aid military recruitment, had passed its topicality when reprinted in 1929. On its republication, Quiller-Couch added a Preface to this effect. The novel had been written at a time of fervent recruitment for the armed forces. The author recalled that recruitment of volunteers faced at least two delicate problems. The rush of volunteers from the Universities, where students had been trained in a sense of private duty, posed one difficulty. The other difficulty concerned the problem of awakening a sense of duty amongst the young men in the countryside, who often contended with consciences that had been informed by the Church's and Chapel's argument that war was anti-Christian. The unthinking actions of those who wrote to newspapers and sent white feathers accusing men who did not enlist of cowardice made the delicate task even more problematic. Quiller-Couch wrote *Nicky-Nan, Reservist* out of resentment over such thoughtless and damaging actions.

Although the eponymous Nicky-Nan, abbreviated from Nicholas Nanjivell, is not a churchgoer, the novel features both church, in the form of High Anglicanism perceived to be "almost hand-in-glove with the Pope" (18), and chapel represented by the kindly but ineffectual Wesleyan minister, Mark Hambly, who spoke ill of no one and listened to no idle gossip (17). The novel concerns Nicky-Nan's initial refusal to enlist, the pressures placed on him as a result, and his eventual march towards the battlefields of Flanders. Like many others who live by the sea, Nicky-Nan is a naval reservist and had not expected to be called to serve in the army. Church and chapel play their parts in Nicky-Nan's story. Hambly's first recorded sermon in the novel follows his selection of a prayer prescribed for use in time of war and tumults from the Book of Common Prayer, and he questions the legitimacy of war waged against people with whom his listeners have no quarrel (47). He describes the slaughter of men by men as horrible and suggests the church's preaching should prevent such horrors by teaching peace on earth and goodwill among people. Although some of the women in the congregation dismiss the sermon as feeble and idiotic and its author as a man in want of a wife to correct him (51), readers believe unequivocally in the preacher's bravery and sincerity.

Soon after the sermon, Nicky-Nan receives a letter from an anonymous well-wisher. Feeling threatened by this letter, he asks Dr. Mant for a certificate vouching for his lack of fitness for service due to a painful swelling on his leg. Because the doctor did not date the letter, it came back by return-post. Nicky-Nan chose to date it himself to save troubling the doctor, and he put off returning it. Through an oversight in the register office, the certificate was not requested until the following year; Nicky-Nan dodged the call-up once again by converting the two of 1912 into a three for 1913. In August 1914, an official letter from the Royal Naval Reserve Registrar arrives in the post which requests information for the reason for Nicky-Nan's noncompliance with the summons to active service. Still not having returned the 1913 forgery, he must provide medical evidence forthwith. Despite pressure from Dr. Mant, who argues that surgery would cure the swelling and would prevent people from accusing Nicky-Nan of being a malingerer who nurses an ailment rather than go to war (165), Nicky-Nan remains adamant in his refusal to report for duty. Pressure increases and includes the allegation that Nicky-Nan serves as a German spy. Ultimately, a Saturday evening recruitment meeting addressed by a speaker from London sways Nicky-Nan's resolution, and he seeks surgery on his leg before enlisting.

Throughout the novel, Quiller-Couch uses the debate between Church and Chapel to highlight the ethics at issue in Nicky-Nan's home town of Polpier. Church and Chapel, Anglicanism and Methodism, agree that an Emergency Committee should be formed in Polpier on the outbreak of war. Plans describe its purposes as caring for the wives and families whose men have gone to war, ensuring they are properly paid and administering the newly-formed relief funds. Agreement on the value of this work brings a degree of truce between the minister and vicar, but this falls apart in the same conversation when the vicar announces that he has sought permission from his bishop to volunteer for military service, not as a chaplain but to fight. Despite the good work of the Emergency Committee, Hambly's general disillusionment with his ministry within the church and his ethical frustrations with what he feels is the breakdown of Christianity leads to his preaching a sermon in which his people understand him to be arguing for the Sunday closure of churches and chapels. He expresses himself as feeling that their "services . . . have lost their point and [their] ministrations their savour" (115). He longs to be useful.

Intellectually torn between commitment to the Gospel of Peace and a response of political pragmatism to the urgent call to fight, the clergymen suffer from the same feelings as those that tear Nicky-Nan apart, though in a less noble manner. Fear may hold Nicky-Nan back, but he receives no censure from Quiller-Couch whose palpable sadness emanates from the final sentence of the novel as Nicky-Nan watches two young men march off to the battlefields of Flanders. Meanwhile, Quiller-Couch holds in quiet admiration the Methodist minister, and others like him, who devote themselves to the Soldiers' and Sailors' Families Association whose main purpose exists to bring relief to the families of those away fighting. It also provides useful tasks for those ineligible to fight, but who want nevertheless to be helpful (144). In testimony to the dependability of Hambly, Nicky-Nan leaves his affairs in the minister's hands when he finally enlists. If, as Quiller-Couch claimed, *Nicky-Nan, Reservist* was one of his tales and romances written in white-hot anger at the authorities' failure to understand the rural and coastal way of thinking, on the assumption that fighting should be left to the professionals, then its result presents a mild-mannered satire of World War I recruitment practices and a sympathetic portrait of its eponymous protagonist and his reluctance to serve. However, the origins of this satirical tale clearly lie in Quiller-Couch's personal credo and doctrine of humanity, as expressed in his unfinished autobiography:

> I believe in the essential goodness of human nature—and my reading backs me—that it has power simply to outlive any doctrine of any Church resorting to any cruelty of enforcement. All the old business of human sacrifice, of God or the gods delighting in the smell of man's fat, of burning heretics, of the devil and his pitchfork, of witches, of the damnation of unbaptized infants—all this and such like yield in the end to no argument, but last only to be dropped aside out of decent men's hearts and minds.[4]

Although a satire, the novel's protagonists are good men doing their best in distressed times.

Forty years later, men like this "grand fellow", Mark Hambly, were in the Reverend Dr. Leslie Weatherhead's mind when he wrote a letter of appreciation to the novelist Howard Spring after the 1955 publication of his book, *These Lovers Fled Away*. Spring's established fame rested on a 1940 novel about a Methodist politician, *Fame is the Spur*, whose story reached the wider public in 1947, when Boulting Brothers made a well-received film of the book starring Michael Redgrave. Weatherhead, a prominent and popular preacher attracting large crowds at the City Temple in London, who served as President of the Methodist Conference in 1955, used his letter to Spring to express appreciation of the earlier novel, then concluded with a suggestion:

> I wish you would write a novel and make a parson the hero—and why not a Methodist parson, for were you not once a local preacher? Parsons are so often effeminate asses, or they commit suicide or they are stupid or obscurantist in modern fiction. The doctors always shine but the poor parson so rarely is a he-man and I know so many grand fellows.[5]

The Boulting Brothers film was received as a record of the demise of the Labour Party in British politics, but the novel, whilst political, provides more of a record of the demise of Methodism and the loss of Methodist ideals. *Fame is the Spur* commences with an account of the funeral of the Old Warrior, a hero of Peterloo from 1819, and thus heralds its Methodist theme from the outset. This focus on Methodism does not surprise, given the deep and lasting influence Methodism had on Spring. According to his wife's biography, Spring's interest in both literary and religious matters had been ignited when he was a boy of twelve, after a lodger left the family home to try his good fortune at starting a new life in South Africa. The lodger left behind a trunk full of books, many of which had belonged to his brother who had died while studying to be a nonconformist minister. The books remained in the Spring household for three years while their absentee owner decided what to do with them. Over these three years, the young Howard avidly worked his way through the small library. The artistry and ideas of the books did not, however, prevent the young Howard from falling under the influence of the Plymouth Brethren, whose chapel stood a stone's throw away from the family home and whose distrust of the literary arts was well-known. Spring attended its Sunday School, but soon realised that this was a wrangling religion, a religion to be saved from, lacking beauty, humility and love. It was a joyless faith, that frowned upon fiction, which was what his wife later called the master-passion of Spring's mind. He was unmoved by the Brethren's predilection towards finding "beams in others' eyes while stridently crowing about the perfection of [their] own spiritual vision."[6] As a teenager, probably when he was thirteen, he left the Brethren unsaved and unbaptised, and "took himself along to the worldly, wicked, music-playing and Amen-chanting Wesleyans."[7] He enjoyed the music there, though his biography notes that the term enjoy has been debased in that it no longer embraces joy and has lost the sense of spiritual exultation. Spring carries this distinction, between the stultifying Plymouth Brethren and the freedom he found in Methodism, into the distinction he makes at Emmott Street Chapel in *Fame is the Spur* between the chapel and the hall where "jollifications that could not be conducted on the more sacred ground floor" took place (72). In contrast with the anti-literary tendencies of the Plymouth Brethren, Spring found himself enchanted by literary pleasures in the Methodist Hymn Book, whose biographical index revealed that he was worshipping in words written by men and women who were, to him, as gods.[8] Poets he revered were the authors of hymns they sang week by week—Alfred Tennyson, Walter Scott, John Milton, Oliver Wendell Holmes, Anne Brontë, Christina Rossetti, William Cowper, Thomas Addison, Charles Kingsley and Ellen Thorneycroft Fowler. In the Methodist chapel, literature he loved was employed in divine worship. What a discovery this was for Spring! It was revelatory; "if God was worshipped by these superlative beings," he wrote, "then God was indeed worshipful."[9]

Methodism proved to be the formative and lasting religious influence on his life, and his autobiography attests to the fact that he drew on his actual experience of the denomination for its representation in *Fame is the*

Spur. For instance, his own observation that Methodist class meetings tended to sort people into social degrees becomes, in the novel, Birley Artingstall's stinging criticism that Wesleyan classes are all graded. Poorer people were grouped in one class whereas anyone with more than five pounds a week did not bother to attend class at all, unless he happened to be a class leader.[10] Nevertheless, Spring attended class meetings for many years, even leading the class during its leader's absences. A dream of his becoming a Methodist minister thus began to emerge, but the cost of attending either Didsbury or Headingley College was prohibitive for a family whose father had been long dead. Instead, he began to train as a Wesleyan local preacher. In his autobiography, he recounts his first sermon given to a congregation of about six or eight people, though he is unable to recall either the text or a single word of the sermon. On his way back from the service through the fields of Llandaff, the Cathedral congregation was streaming out into the dusky night, and he thought how different that congregation was to the one he had just led in worship. He could not allow himself to think that one day he might address a larger crowd than eight. Although he stayed on the Methodist plan for four years until he moved to Bradford, with hindsight he reckons he had never seriously entertained the thought that he might become a parson.[11] Looking back on his years as a local preacher, he borrows a Scottish term to describe himself as "stickit" from which it can be inferred that he regarded himself as plodding and unsuccessful in the pulpit. In Bradford, he attended a Wesleyan church, but he no longer led services. When he moved to Manchester in the early days of the First World War, his church-going days ended. His involvement in Methodism for about a decade of his earlier years gave him a well-informed understanding of the denomination, to such an extent that his portrayal of Methodists in his fiction rings true to reality.

The strength of the Methodist focus in the early chapters of *Fame is the Spur* accentuates the demise of Methodism and Methodist ideals described in its later pages. The novel concerns John Hamer Shawcross's rise from a humble Methodist home in Manchester to the rank of Cabinet Minister. Known as John as a boy, as a man he adopts his middle name, Hamer. The narrative technique of having a mature man recall a childhood memory in which his grandfather spoke of his own youth allows the opening chapter to bridge over one hundred years of history and refer to a formative event in Methodist history. The mature Hamer's memory of his grandfather's funeral, the so-called Old Warrior, who shared the boy's bedroom in his childhood home, where a sabre hung over the mantelshelf, pours into his mind, spurred by his attendance at a Cenotaph memorial as a government minister. The Old Warrior's funeral takes the reader back to 1819, the year of the Peterloo Massacre, where the grandfather was a veteran of the workers' resistance to government action on that fateful day. He collected the sabre when it fell in the field of conflict, and, but for chance, he might have killed a soldier with it. Thereafter, he kept it as a souvenir that became a complex symbol, not only representing resistance to oppression, but also the biblical warning that those who take up the sword die by the sword, an admonition that leads to commitment to peace. It enabled the Old Warrior to elaborate the truth of his part in the action, and it stood as a representation of "a condition of warfare existing between two sets of men" (24), the perennial class struggle. The Peterloo Massacre, when cavalry charged into a crowd demonstrating their demand of parliamentary reform, divided Methodists; some believed that Methodist leaders had failed their people when they supported the government in the aftermath of the events, while others thought that support for the authorities was appropriate. Peterloo defined a moment in the history of the working classes. Feeling that a hearse, a cab and a small wreath of yellow chrysanthemums make a small and ignoble tribute to an aged veteran of Peterloo, Shawcross's mother hurriedly places the sabre on the Old Warrior's coffin and, after the funeral, Shawcross is allowed to keep it for himself. This reminder of radical origins of working class politics will accompany him throughout his political career. As an establishment figure at the Cenotaph, he remembers it, and this memory introduces Spring's narrative of a boy's upbringing in a Manchester Methodist home.

The home is that of Gordon Stansfield, a Wesleyan local preacher, who had charitably taken in Ellen Shawcross and her illegitimate son when everyone else had cold-shouldered them, thus providing both with a home and the mother with a stable environment for the upbringing of her boy. Religion is dutifully practised in the home with grace said at each meal and a certain routine and ritual about preparing for church in that Saturday night served as Gordon's sermon-writing night. Even though he was not called on to preach every Sunday, Gordon invariably worked on a sermon each Saturday after the ritual of clearing the kitchen so that it could become a study. A blotting-pad, ink-pot, and pen were taken from the drawer, a sheaf of half-sheets of paper was placed alongside a Bible, a *Cruden's Concordance*, and *The Methodist Hymn Book* before silence descended on the kitchen, and Gordon worked.

Services at Emmott Street Wesleyan Chapel seem equally formulaic. Gordon's friend and employer is Birley Artingstall who "endured" everything about the service—the anthem and hymns, sermon, announcements and collection—with patience because he was waiting for the prayer-meeting that followed. He lived for the moment when the minister said, "Perhaps Brother Birley Artingstall will lead us to the mercy seat." Then he would stand and pour out "petitions that once had had the virtue of extempore utterance but now were polished and rehearsed litanies" (36). In these early scenes, Spring is portraying Methodism as no longer being the force it once was. What had been spontaneous is now reduced to performance.

Nevertheless, church culture retains the capacity to cut into personal relationships and Gordon encourages Shawcross to befriend Arnold Ryerson. Once, when the boys are together at Gordon's home, Gordon suggests they pray, and he leads the boys in a prayer for their friendship that it may grow into a sustaining colleagueship that gives glory to God (60).

The class meeting was one of the distinguishing characteristics of Methodism from the time of the Wesleys until the middle years of the twentieth century when fewer Methodists met in such groups. In the early years, class meetings functioned like cell groups or self-help groups of mutual encouragement, as their members met weekly under the pastoral oversight of a class leader. At each meeting, members were expected to give an account of God's work within them since they last met. Prayer for each other, celebration of God's work in those who were flourishing, and concern for those who were backsliding formed a large part of the meeting, although there was also time and space for Bible study and teaching. As decades passed, the class meeting evolved into a less demanding form of pastoral care, with class leaders functioning as pastoral visitors and with fewer, or even no, actual meetings of the group. All church members were still assigned a class leader who distributed their membership tickets quarterly. British Methodists, in the first decades of the twenty-first century, still receive an annual membership card distributed by their assigned pastoral visitor. Spring wrote *Fame is the Spur* at a time when many Methodist churches were worrying that the class meeting was in demise because fewer classes met, but the action of the novel occurs both in an earlier time and in a traditionalist region of Britain where class meetings were stronger. His depiction of them is sufficiently authentic to show the author's first-hand knowledge of their structure and function. Hamer Shawcross's mother had never become a member of the church and did not, therefore, attend class meetings, but she is happy for Gordon to take her son to his class, unorthodox though this is. Gordon may have spotted the evangelistic opportunities provided by the class, as well as its intended faith development. As he sets off to attend class, Ellen Shawcross slips a penny into her son's hand, but Spring dissipates any potential excitement about the possible effects attending the class might have on the boy by telling readers of the formidable prison-like railings around the chapel which stood like "a blackened fortress" over which grey clouds had wept sooty tears so that all was as "black and funereal as crape" (72). The path to the door passed through sour-looking earth, "sterile and poisonous soil" in which only a few elder trees grew. They by-passed the locked, stout oak, nail-studded front door to pass through a basement door into a cheerless dimly-lit space, where the members assembled. Primarily women from poor homes, they had all left their younger children at home in the charge of elder children, but once the meeting was underway the room lit up a little as the congregation sang an easy, popular, and harmonious Charles Wesley hymn with gusto. In the setting of that dull room, the singing sounded cheerless, timid, thin, and eerie. Gordon, as class leader, began a quiet, simple prayer, from which the emotional, showy fervour evident at prayer meetings was absent. Because he had brought along two new members to the meeting, Gordon explained the purpose of the class—a place for personal confessions and personal testimony, not a place for sermons or long addresses, but a safe environment for mutual comfort and encouragement, as John Wesley intended (74). Shawcross observed that what followed was obviously a well-understood routine of each in turn making confession, asking for prayers or giving testimony, but some were allowed to remain silent. Each name was called and each laid a penny on the table. When Shawcross handed his penny over, Spring records that the young boy was perplexed by the meeting, which had seemed dreary and wearying, in defiant resistance to the joy with which Gordon had gone to the meeting, and which was still evident on his face (76). The class meeting then concluded with a hymn Gordon had carefully chosen, a hymn praying for Jesus' protection for his little ones that they may be safe from the prowling snares of Satan.

The hymn's prayer expresses something of Gordon's plan for Hamer Shawcross; he hopes the boy will become a preacher. In the Stansfield home, he furnishes Hamer with a study with a writing-table and book shelves. Gordon supplied books for the shelves, among which were *Birds of the Bible*, Southey's *Life of Wesley* and a volume of John Wesley's sermons, remarking as he placed the latter on the shelves, "If either of you lads ever takes to local preaching [...] you'll want this. You've got to be well up in some of these sermons, you know, before they'll accept you" (62). More books are added later, to such an extent that, by the time Hamer was fifteen, he "had had his eyes opened in many directions" (84). Even reading a book as stolid as Wesley's *Journal* became, for the young boy, an armchair travel adventure. On his fourteenth birthday, Gordon makes his hopes explicit when he tells Hamer he hopes the boy will become either a minister or a local preacher one day. Both Birley Artingstall and, later, Robert Wilder, share this obsession to make a minister of Hamer. Gordon, teasingly, addresses him as "The Reverend J. Hamer Shawcross." The boy likes the sound of this so much that, from then on, he styles himself as J. Hamer Shawcross and is known no longer as John but as Hamer. He quite likes the sound of the title, too (88).

Within *Fame is the Spur,* by juxtaposing the formative spiritual and religious experiences of three young characters, Spring causes readers to question their integrity. These are the experiences of Harriet Wilder, the daughter of a new parson, of Ann Artingstall, Birley's daughter, alongside whom Hamer has grown up, and of Hamer himself. Harriet impresses Hamer when they socialise after the church service. The persuasiveness of the Reverend Robert Wilder's sermon enticed Hamer to stay for Holy Communion. Post-worship service Communion, practised in the Methodist Church as an addendum to the main service in the first three quarters of the twentieth century, allowed non-communicant members to leave prior to its observance. This scene enacts Hamer's first Communion and, invited to the manse for supper afterwards, he talks quietly with Harriet while the main conversation takes place among the adults around the table. She tells of the places where she has lived as her father moved from circuit to circuit, and she expresses her intention to stay with her father since he was widowed despite her long-held ambition to be a medical missionary in India. Ann Artingstall impresses the reader with her radical commitment to relief of the poor, the result of first-hand experience of poverty when she visits the Ryerson home. She is much more principled than Hamer as a child, even to the point of rejecting the influence of her parents. In contrast with these young Methodist women, Hamer's progress within the Methodist Church continues, spurred by something other than either loyal duty or principled devotion to a cause. One of Hamer's diary entries betrays his true motives. Encouraged by Gordon to emulate the example of Charles Haddon Spurgeon, a prominent Free Church preacher of the era who began his preaching in his teenage years, Hamer prepares a short sermon for the class meeting, but only after he has heard a guest preacher at the Chapel Anniversary who preached such a good sermon that during the following hymn the fervour of the singing reflected the power of the preaching. In his diary, Hamer writes, "Then I wished again that I was the preacher, because it must be very fine to have a great congregation in the hollow of your hand" (139). The sermon he gives in the class meeting conflicts with the usual ethos of the meeting. He gives a survey of his own achievements, an exposition of an austere doctrine of self-improvement with a mere nod in the direction of dependency upon God. When he did mention his hunger for God, Spring reckons Hamer knew nothing of spiritual hunger (156). If the text of this sermon had survived it would have been fodder to feed the fire of criticism levelled later by his political enemies, because its general import was: "Ah, my friends, see what a good boy am I" (157).

Indubitably, Hamer was studious and followed the guidance of his mentors, both Gordon and Birley, who advise him on his reading, which is primarily socialist and Christian. Significantly, when he reads Milton, lines from *Lycidas* run like an earworm through his mind, lines which form one of the novel's two epigraphs and from which the novel's title is taken:

> Fame is the spur that the clear spirit doth raise
> (That last infirmity of the noble mind)
> To scorn delights and live laborious days.

"Fame" is the word buzzing in his head for days (147). Despite the suggestion that Spring chose the title for his book as a pun on the last phrase of these lines, given that Hamer Shawcross serves as a Labour politician and thus lived laborious days, the novel primarily serves as a satire on the corrupting power of the ambition to be famous. Throughout Hamer's early years, his Christian service had been characterised by a look-at-me attitude, and this mental attitude drives him on. For instance, when Harriet Wilder congratulated Hamer on his first sermon, she expresses high regard for her own father. She over-estimates her father's scholarship and says that, unlike many Wesleyan parsons, he is a great scholar (196). This comment leads Hamer to the realisation that this is what he wants to be, too. As a general practice, for much of the twentieth century, the Methodist Church prided itself on having a low academic threshold for admission to the presbyterate on the basis of the belief and principle that God can call anyone. The Church had greater regard for candidates' ability as preachers than for academic qualifications, so accreditation as a local preacher was the main prerequisite for acceptance by the Church for pre-ordination training, and trial services determined a candidates' suitability throughout the process. That Harriet had an exaggerated opinion of her father, who, for instance, could only get by in Hebrew, did not, however, deter Hamer from his scholarly ambitions.

His studies fuelled his preaching, and, from the beginning, he was popular. His mother marvelled at his sermons in a way she did not when Gordon Stansfield preached. Wilder told her that he had never heard a young preacher with such a powerful gift, but she secretly harboured a doubt: "the easy brilliance, the challenging eye, the persuasive gestures and the rise and fall of the voice that could plead, condemn [and] exhort" suggest artistry and theatricality that borders on affected histrionics and troubles the integrity of the preacher (204-5). Hamer's sermons did not touch her heart as Gordon's simple godliness did. The "here I am: look at me" aspect of his preaching challenges his integrity, in a manner reminiscent of another literary preacher, the parson in Thomas Hardy's poem "In Church." In this poem the parson, who has just mesmerised and thrilled a packed church with his sermon, rehearses his moves in the vestry afterwards, only to be caught by a pupil whose admiration for the preacher immediately dissipates.[12] The theatricality of both Hardy's preacher and Hamer Shawcross compromise what they have to say. Hamer's self-consciousness in the sermon he preaches at the Watchnight Service, a typical Methodist tradition on New Year's Eve, now more neglected than observed, establishes a pattern for his preaching and, later, for his political oratory:

> It was a simple address, obvious as the daylight, as all his addresses then were; but it had the quality of his personality behind it. He was more and more, at this time, savouring his life as an adventure towards he knew not what ... And so he was able to impart to his audience something of this driving confidence in life, this challenge to lions in the path that proved to be only chained lions, this belief that though ye have not passed this way heretofore, ye shall pass, and come out safely on the other side. (208)

Later in his diary, he sets himself apart from those he led in worship, remarking that for them the following year would hold nothing other than whatever the dying year had held, whilst he senses great things in his own life. He shows no desire to improve the people's lot; his greater interest is in "the exercise of this gift of speech" (313).

Nevertheless, *Fame is the Spur* focuses on a politician, not a parson. Hamer's career, but perhaps not his vocation, concerns serving as a Labour Member of Parliament, yet the grounding Hamer's Methodist upbringing gave to his career assumes importance in this study of Methodists in fiction. He has read Samuel Johnson's *Vanity of Human Wishes*, and his vanity as an orator spurs his preaching. When the author describes Hamer as a young politician, "preach[ing] from his soapbox" (271), Spring establishes an equivalence between religious faith and political action with which actual early Methodists would have been comfortable, but his political rhetoric does not stand up to analysis. For instance, giving a speech on the housing question, he attempts the

Aristotelian rhetorical technique of establishing an emotional state of friendliness with his auditors, winning their empathy by referring to previous personal hardship:

> I was condemned to live in a shack, a hovel, with rude winds whistling in at the door, but, thank God, with the clean free sky above me speaking with the immortal encouragement of the stars (272).

The truth of these claims is dubious, and Spring wryly comments that no one was quite sure what the last phrase meant, but that did not matter when Hamer was riding his oratorical mount. Does the substance of his political rhetoric matter any more than the religious rhetoric of preaching? For Hamer, perhaps not. Years later, he teaches his son, Charles, that big words are grand things; "[t]hey can be like coronation robes on a piddling little king" (435). Well-chosen words and carefully-crafted speeches can make nothing much sound very important. As a mature politician, Hamer does not surrender his past entirely: biblical vocabulary and imagery inform both his political decisions and his speeches. Four examples suffice as evidence. First, in the early stages of his career, in the glow of victory at the end of the First World War, when a general election sought a mandate to continue with the Coalition Government, Hamer urged the Labour Party to withdraw using the biblical injunction: "Come ye out from among them and be ye separate" (511). He lost his own seat in Parliament. Second, internal party struggles did not faze him; he grandly saw his arguments with individual politicians who disagreed with him as his struggle "against principalities and powers, against darkness in high places" (514). Third, when announcing his intention to seek a return to Parliament, his political speeches deployed the linguistic repertoire of the Flood narrative in the Book of Genesis:

> I have been out like Noah's dove scanning the face of the waters. Now I come back, and ah! my friends, I do not come back with an olive branch. The waters are not abated ... Our ark is still adrift; the rain of misfortune still pelts. (534)

Fourth, when Hamer and Arnold travel on the hustings, he preaches the vision of Revelation 21, actually taking a Bible from his pocket and placing it on the lectern before reading, "I saw a new heaven and a new earth" (327). Instances like these lead one of his acquaintances in the dying embers of his political life to remark that, whenever they meet, Hamer treats her to a sermon. He reminds her he was once a local preacher (624). The influence of preacher training had been deep and lasting; the relationship between his religion and his politics, though distorted, is never lost.

Spring, who uses hymns in the novel as markers in the political story, possessed full awareness of the centrality of hymn singing to Methodist worship and of hymns to Methodist spirituality. One Christmas, Birley Artingstall hosted a family gathering. As he lit the brandy over the Christmas pudding, he promised they would sing carols after dinner. The satiated quietness after dinner resembled prayer-like tranquillity. Then they sang hymn after hymn, without needing to consult the index of the Methodist Hymn Book to find them, as they were all so familiar to them. After they had sung "Let Earth and Heaven Combine," a Christmas hymn of Charles Wesley's, second only to "Hark, the Herald Angels Sing" in popularity among Methodists, Birley sat back in his chair, laid down the pipe with which he had been conducting the singing and said, "You young people have all been talking about reforming this and reforming that. Well, it's all there in two lines. When men love one another, all the reforms will be over. There's no other way" (174). He referred to the two last lines of the hymn's final flourish:

> Then shall His love be fully showed
> And man shall then be lost in God.

Religious fulfilment and political fulfilment are one for these Methodists; heaven on earth is their political goal, as much as it is the object of their prayers. Hamer's diary reflects on the successful and memorable speech he made early in his political career in St Swithin's, which some say was his greatest speech (329). He had ended it by speaking of Labour's crusade for universal peace, and the audience's response was to stand to sing

> These things shall be! A loftier race
> Than e'er the world have known shall rise,
> With flame of freedom in their souls
> And light of knowledge in their eyes.
>
> New arts shall bloom of loftier mould,
> And mightier music thrill the skies
> And every life shall be a song
> When all the earth is paradise.

The story of this hymn, usually sung to a stirring tune such as Truro, as set in The Methodist Hymn Book of 1933, says that its author, John Addlington Symonds, saw it as a depiction of a regenerated world, and "A Regenerated World" is the subtitle he gave it. In Christian terms, it speaks of a world lifted out of its bondage to squalor into the beauty of freedom, education, fine arts and uplifting music. The song dreams of the socialist republic established through political campaigning, often in those days accompanied by hymn singing. Welsh miners, for instance, campaigning in London for better working conditions, trudged the Strand "wailing those dolorous, heart-breaking hymns of the Welsh" (276), such as "Jesu, Lover of My Soul." The tune, Aberystwyth, is Welsh, but the author is English—Charles Wesley. Spring's use of hymns in *Fame is the Spur* accords with Methodist practice. They carried their hymn books to chapel, read their hymns in their private devotions, quoted them in their sermons, and sang them where and whenever they sang, because their lyrical theology expressed their deep longing for God and their hope for God's Kingdom on earth. Their hymnody taught them their belief.

The tragedy of *Fame is the Spur* lies in the death of the dream that fuelled the political ambitions of Hamer Shawcross, and some of his fellows. A total sense of tragedy in the novel is prevented, however, by the dream's lack of clarity. What, after all, was Hamer's dream? Was it a Methodist dream born in the chapel, a socialist dream born among the deprived lives of Manchester's working class, or a dream of personal power and fame spurred by misplaced ambition? Readers know only his words; challenged in his later years about whether he remembers the dreams of his youth, he protests, "What do you know about my dreams? . . . You know only my words. My words have been for others. Am I not allowed a dream for myself?" (592). The less-than-omniscient third person narrator, who nonetheless knows more than the reader, later says that Hamer's political career had been stimulated by his belief in "perfectability, in a loftier race, the light of knowledge, the flame of freedom, Jerusalem in England's green and pleasant land" (610), a blend of Wesleyan, Blakean and socialist doctrines. Yet, there are those around Hamer who, at the close of his political career, feel betrayed because he has deserted this cause of beauty and glory. Such binary simplicity is insufficient for Spring. At the novel's dénouement, he adds another dimension. As the old man's life comes to an end, his faith snuffs out like a candle in a hurricane, for it seems that the entire world is embattled. The nations were descending into war once more. So, Spring asks, does anyone find their dreams fulfilled (669)? The despondency within Spring's question presents no surprise. He may have completed the novel in 1938, shortly after the Spanish Civil War, a war that dashed so many ideals. Or, he may have completed it nearer its publication date of 1940, by which time the world was at war with itself. Uncertainty about the completion date remains. Either way, these were difficult days for hopes and dreams.

Hamer ends his life with the drone of aircraft vibrating in the sky, yet still able to hear above them his own voice as an innocent, as yet unspoilt, child. If his dreams were dead, at least he could be near their ghosts. The damning verdict on his political life, given by his own son Charles, that he "who once demanded the Millennium had settled for Pleasant Sunday Afternoons" (646) is memorable, but it is not the last word. Despite all his mistakes and his arrogance, there remains a mark of nobility and principle within Hamer Shawcross. Some of his elegance establishes itself by the significant intertexts of the novel: Milton's *Lycidas*, Blake's *Jerusalem*, Charles Wesley's hymnody, the new heaven and new earth of *The Book of Revelation* and Symonds's *These Things Shall Be!* In one of the last conversations Hamer and Ann Artingstall share, Ann recites some lines from George Herbert's poem, *The Priesthood*, in which the poet wittily uses the Old Testament parable of the potter in Jeremiah's prophecy. Herbert imagines that the potter might one day want to show off his skill by working on particularly unpromising clay. The lines Ann quotes are the last three of the poem's penultimate stanza and the first three of the last:

> Only since God doth often vessels make
> Of lowly matter for high uses meet,
> I throw me at His feet;
> There will I lie until my Maker seek
> For some mean stuff whereon to show His skill,
> Then is my time.

Hamer appreciates the beauty of these words (517), but their presence in this conversation comes as accusation; Hamer has not humbly laid himself at God's feet waiting for God to work in and through him. The tragedy of the novel demonstrates that he has not stood firm in his Christian principles.

No one would be foolish enough to suggest that all Methodists of the twentieth century flew on mercy's wings to offer ready aid to the poor and helpless. No one would be foolish enough to suggest that all Methodists of the twentieth century were principled men and women. Of course, there have been notable and praiseworthy examples of men and women from the Methodist chapels whose public service, in politics, in welfare, in charities, and in voluntary work has transformed lives, but many have been like Quiller-Couch's Mark Hambly and Spring's Hamer Shawcross, flawed servants of God and humankind. When we ask whether fictional Methodism of the twentieth century has a real political and social impact, when we ask if it is seen to transform people's lives and lift them above drudgery and want, when we ask whether these novels provide a sense of true religion as Charles Wesley saw it in his hymn beginning "Jesus, the Gift Divine I Know," readers cannot avoid the conclusion that, in this respect, tragic novels are, in their tragic elements, faithful to Methodism as it really is.

CHAPTER FOUR

ENOUGH FOR EVERMORE

Two nonconformist denominations feature in Iris Murdoch's *The Philosopher's Pupil* (1983). One is the Society of Friends, or Quakers, represented by William Eastcote, also known as Bill the Lizard. Of him, nothing ill is said. The other is Methodism represented by the titular philosopher, John Robert Rozanov whose return from America with his granddaughter triggers the novel's action. The author portrays Rozanov as more ambivalent than Eastcote. Rozanov's upbringing in a Methodist home had little effect on his academic interests as a philosopher, but it had "made of him a puritan with an obsessive guilt-ridden sense of truth" (134). The novel's third-person narrator, who appears occasionally as a character in the book and knows Rozanov well, declares him incapable of swearing, vulgarity, lying or deceit (135). However, in the unreliability of the narrator's judgement lies the novel's flaw, for Rozanov's return to Ennistone is an entire pretence. Rozanov organises accommodation for his granddaughter, known both as Harriet and Hattie, in Slipper House with her maid. Soon thereafter, he arranges for Tom McCaffrey to visit her, having sworn Tom to secrecy about his bizarre intention to arrange for Harriet and Tom to marry. Although Tom, a "pretty boy," wants to be loved by everyone and is initially open to Rozanov's machinations, the narrator's judgement that Rozanov is incapable of deceit is put into question by his actions.

When Tom, a relatively uncomplicated man who finds himself unable to sustain forced conversation, fails to carry out the subterfuge amid the complexities of unorthodox relationships, Rozanov is outraged and, fearing both that his underhand deal with Tom will be exposed to Hattie and that her future is now uncertain, he reveals the motives behind his actions in declaring that he is incestuously in love with Hattie "even if it makes [her] shudder, even if it makes [her] run" (470). She seeks clarification: does he love her "like grandfather or like being in love?" (463). He loves her as a lover would, and his efforts to arrange a safe marriage for her had been an attempt to control her life and keep her close.

Murdoch's assertion that Methodism had made Rozanov serious-minded and intense, as well as strict in his high expectations of others, permits readers to question whether other aspects of his behaviour stemmed from his Methodist childhood. Might it also have deluded him and rendered him obsessively and sexually attracted to his own granddaughter? Murdoch treats too insufficiently the nature of the Methodism Rozanov experienced either to establish any link between what he was taught and his later behaviour or to explain the inconsistency in his character. She, like other novelists of recent decades, has merely used Methodism as shorthand for strict and unattractive nonconformity in contrast with the so-called better expression of nonconformist religion found among the Quakers. Murdoch exploits all of Rozanov's imperfections to pose the novel's overarching question, namely whether any form of philosophy or religion can save humankind from its depravity.

The answer to this question which the novel asks readers to consider achieves personification in the form of the local priest, Father Bernard, who had long since ceased believing in God (155), but who now stands as a bridge between Christianity and Buddhism, to which Murdoch was strongly attracted. His spiritual practice took a form of unorthodox meditation as he sat facing Buddha and listened to the music of Scott Joplin (506). The novel's epilogue, entitled "What Happened Afterwards," includes a letter from Father Bernard in which he writes that only true religion can save the human race and that, although there is no God, a role remains for godless religion in human society and individual lives. For the second time in her novels, Murdoch employs the concept of an atheistic sermon. On the first occasion, in *The Time of the Angels* (1966), the priest, Carel Fisher, is repeatedly tempted to announce from the pulpit that there is no God. Murdoch uses this novel to open up an exploration of the concept of God as Good, but Carel Fisher felt his vocation to be a priest of no God. Following this model, at the conclusion of *The Philosopher's Pupil*, Father Bernard writes in his letter that he has discovered his true vocation as one who has been chosen to strive for the continuance of religion on earth but his life has taken an eremitical turn, as he lives now in a cave, a tiny abandoned chapel, near Mount Athos. A few local villagers bring him food most days. When they come, he preaches to them; when they don't appear, he preaches to the birds that "there is no God, that even the beauty of Christ is a snare and a lie" (570).

Father Bernard's preaching sounds bitter, when contrasted with that of the novel's model Quaker, William Eastcote, whose address in a Quaker meeting began with the notion that we live in an age of marvels, included encouragement for his hearers to lead simple, orderly, open, and truthful lives. His plea ended with a conventional exhortation, "Recognise one's own evil, mend what can be mended, and for what cannot be undone, place it in love and faith in the clear light of the healing goodness of God" (204-5). But, the context of the novel indicates that the sermon has an intended positive aspect. Father Bernard does not dismiss religion, but denies its supernatural reality; he does not dismiss the practice of religion, but argues for a rationalist demythologised religion that does not name God other than Good. The theology assumed in such religious practices may be regarded as atheology. Father Bernard advocates what Murdoch calls "charmless holiness" (572) as the form of religion that can rescue humanity from whatever ails it. Far removed from the teachings and practices of both the Church of England in which Father Bernard is ordained and the Methodist Church in which the novel's philosopher was reared, the fact remains that the novel accords more value to Quakerism than it does to either Methodism or Anglicanism. Opportunities for the novel to engage in dialogue between the formal Anglican and Methodist religious practices and the alternative that Father Bernard represents are missed. Nevertheless, Father Bernard possesses greater persuasiveness than another of Murdoch's fictional priests, Father McAllister in *The Book and the Brotherhood* (1987), who also struggles to keep the faith and understanding of God he inherited from his Anglican father and the understanding of Christ he inherited from his Methodist mother. McAllister's austere God, before whom the human soul shivers like a moth (575), and his demanding Christ lead him to coerce an impressionable parishioner, Tamar, into an insincere and unscrupulous religious conversion.

Murdoch's use of Methodism in her novels demonstrates its literary diminution to little more than a convenient cipher for repressive religious conservatism or puritanical hypocrisy. Can this be also true of other Methodist novels?

Contrasting with Murdoch's uncomplimentary portrait of Methodists, J. L. Carr's nostalgic depiction in his novella, *A Month in the Country* (1980), shows he holds the denomination in much higher esteem. According to Penelope Fitzgerald's introduction to the Penguin Classics edition of the book, the author's father had been a Wesleyan local preacher. The young Carr would often play truant from chapel, yet his memory of revivalist hymns was indelible. However, the hymns Fitzgerald cites—"Hold The Fort," "Count Your Blessings," "Pull For The Shore, Sailor," and "We Are Out On the Ocean Sailing"—are all gospel hall-type songs rather than hymns likely to be sung in Methodist chapels. This brings into question Fitzgerald's identification of Carr's father as Wesleyan, for these hymns suggest that the chapels in which Carr's father preached were more likely to be Primitive than Wesleyan. Fitzgerald's misidentification of Carr's father is another example of a non-Methodist seeing no need to distinguish the various groupings within Methodism. To some extent, this confusion carries over into the novel, for the chapel Carr describes is named Wesleyan but bears the hallmarks of a lay-led Primitive fellowship.

Told by Tom Birkin, a shell-shocked First World War survivor, Carr's novella, *A Month in the Country*, recounts Birkin's work, in 1920, on the restoration of a medieval fresco. Told by the restorer himself from the chronological perspective of 1978, the reader learns that the trauma of the war left Birkin with a disfiguring facial tick resulting from injury at Passchendaele and post-traumatic stress that brought his marriage to the brink of collapse. Tom tells of his retreat to the tranquil surroundings of Oxgodby in Yorkshire where he busies himself with work which he finds therapeutic. Restoration of the fresco provides restoration for him, as well. The summer of 1920, when he spends the month in the country, becomes "a haven of calm water" for him (12) but, when he reflects on it nearly sixty years later, he realises that "it's gone" (14). Such is the nature of the past; what is good about it can easily be left behind, but its worst aspects leave scars. The quiet church and the slowly-reappearing picture are simultaneously and paradoxically dream-like and real, and this combination of work and rest proves restorative for Tom. The concentration of labour, carried out in peaceful surroundings, begins to repair his soul, and Oxgodby felt like a latter-day Eden (33).

The fresco Tom restores, a medieval depiction of the last judgment, spurs a conversation about hell with Alice Keach, who comes one day to see him at work. Unsurprisingly, Tom expresses belief in hell because he has seen it. As was the case for many who survived the 1914-18 war, the horrors of battle, the huge numbers of casualties and fatalities, and the nightmarish scenes that continued to haunt those who experienced them were hell-like for Tom. "The world made mud" (59) was not the aching timeless hell of the Bible, yet Tom knows this hell because he had journeyed there and had a map of it in his head. He needed to escape this hell on earth, and village Methodism has a part to play in his recovery.

Upon first arriving at Oxgodby railway station, Tom meets Ellerbeck, the stationmaster, and his fourteen-year-old daughter who takes a shine to him and visits him almost daily. Soon, Ellerbeck extends an invitation for Tom to come to lunch when the Ellerbecks host a visiting preacher with whom conversation often does not flow easily. Ellerbeck believes that Tom and the preacher will get on well together. Carr's readers learn that the Wesleyan chapel had different preachers each week, many of whom gave lively performances. Often their preaching was "rough stuff," their sermons not particularly well-crafted, yet usually delivered with firm conviction. Their difficulty persists because none of these preachers had homiletic training and little to guide them other than that which they had witnessed among their predecessors; "each purveyor of the gospel had no exemplar other than some earlier preacher he had admired" (43). The mild-mannered Ellerbeck, for instance, became like his violently irrational father in the pulpit. Although Tom had not attended church since he was a boy, he becomes caught up in the Ellerbecks' chapel-going habit because of the standing invitation he had to supper at their home. One Sunday, Ellerbeck has a double preaching appointment in two different chapels which would require a brisk and lengthy bicycle ride after the afternoon service to arrive in time for the evening service. At Mrs. Ellerbeck's suggestion, Ellerbeck, too tired to take both (52), sends Tom to take the evening service, assuring him only two or three people will attend and that God will put words into his mouth (53).

Indeed, only a small congregation gathers. Tom's recollection of his first and only experience of leading worship and preaching provides amusement for the reader; he asks the organist to choose long hymns with choruses between each verse and he finds two long chapters, one from each of the Old and New Testaments, to fill out the service and reduce the amount of personal contribution required of him. He gives his hearers permission to nod off or leave if they wish and speaks to them about what he was doing in the church at Oxgodby. Contrary to his expectations, they seem interested in his work, ask several intelligent questions, and promise to drive over to see the restored fresco. The entire experience teaches him that he does not feel cut out to be a preacher, and that realisation leads to an atheistic outburst heard by none but the reader. As Tom walks back to Oxgodby, by a dyke-side on an empty road, he curses the governments that led the nations to war, "Oh you bastards, you awful bloody bastards! You didn't need to have started it. And you could have stopped it before you did. God? Ha! There is no God" (55). This outburst helps him turn a corner in his recuperation.

After his month in the country, Tom never revisited Oxgodby. Because of the retrospective quality of Tom's narrative, told after the passage of fifty-eight years, nostalgia for a lost, distant past looms as an inevitable constituent of Carr's novel. Its narrator yearns for a time when he felt at home and at peace with himself. Yet, what Carr presents is more complex than a pastoral idyll. Oxgodby remains as Tom left it in his memory as "a sealed room furnished by the past, airless, still" (85). Even if it were possible, to go back there would be suffocating; the month in Oxgodby, once cathartic, no longer serves life.

Fuller in his description of early-twentieth century Methodism than Iris Murdoch, Carr nevertheless does not eulogise. Although Tom Birkin's mixed experience of village Methodism drove him to deny God, it contributed to a recovery sufficient for him to return to his home and family. So Carr's readers might ask whether he, too, as the truanting son of a Wesleyan preacher, had mixed feelings about his family religion. Did he think of the Methodist Church, like blue-remembered Oxgodby, as asphyxiating, airless and still? Or could it continue to bear the promise of renewal of hope and belief in a complex postmodern world where competing religious convictions vie for truth and validity?

Two other British novelists, who reserve a prominent place for Methodism, despite writing for readers whose actual experience of the denomination is severely limited, are Peter Hobbs and Barry Unsworth. Their novels, respectively *The Short Day Dying* (2005) and *The Quality of Mercy* (2011), depict the Methodism of a bygone age, not unusual since no British novels of the last twenty-five years depict contemporary Methodism.

In *The Short Day Dying*, a preacher, young Charles Wenmoth, represents Methodism. A Cornishman training to be a local preacher, he regularly visits Harriet French, a young blind tubercular woman who dies before he is able to declare his love for her. Her death, in 1870, makes his circumstances gloomy. Not only does loneliness threaten to overwhelm him in the grievous aftermath of his bereavement, but also congregations dwindle and his faith gutters like a candle whose flame flickers to the point of extinguishment. An interiorised novel, *The Short Day Dying* takes the form of a spiritual journal, whose model is either Augustinian, in that it reminds readers of Augustine of Hippo's *Confessions*, or Augustan in that it is reminiscent of *Augustus Carp by Himself*, the early twentieth-century parody of earnest Victorian spiritual autobiographies.

Most reviewers remark on one obvious feature of the novel, the absence of all punctuation except full stops. While this seems to be an idiosyncratic way for Hobbs to establish the authenticity of an unschooled journal, Hobbs has explained the significance of this stylistic technique.[1] Hobbs deliberately did little research beyond looking at old photographs for information about the style of clothes worn and the range of food eaten in the era as well as some circuit preaching plans for regional surnames. But he did have one key primary source, two diaries belonging to an ancestor who was the real figure behind the fictional Wenmoth. Deciphering these had occupied Hobbs's father for several years. Primarily comprised of a dull day-to-day account of a rather humdrum life, often doing little more than listing the Bible texts for sermons he had heard, the diaries occasionally, however, achieved a more poetic voice. Hobbs remembers one place where, instead of writing, "Another week is past," his ancestor wrote, "Another Sabbath is gone into eternity." These became the opening words of the novel, in which, from then on, this ill-educated, yet poetic, voice recounts the narrative.

Bringing the Methodist features of this novel to the foreground in this study risks distorting the text, for Hobbs did not set out to write a religious or historical novel. His themes, contemporary and universal, dealt with "the passing of time and the inaccessibility of the past, doubt (and not particularly religious doubt), consciousness, the extent to which we are free to make our lives, the narratives we have about ourselves that don't quite match reality and the phenomenology of suffering."[2] He chose, however, to explore these themes against the backdrop of the historical religious context of nineteenth-century Cornish Methodism. Cornish scenery and Cornish Methodist culture were "twin canvases" for Hobbs to work on, as well as the background to Hobbs's own childhood. Since both his parents were Methodist local preachers, initially in rural Cornwall before the family moved to North Yorkshire, Hobbs remembers accompanying one or other of them to preach at small chapels where there might be as few as three or four people attending the service. These experiences helped him to imagine Wenmoth's services.

Like Hobbs's ancestor's diaries, Wenmoth's year-long spiritual autobiography contains many references to sermons and their Bible texts, making the novel both a book about speaking as well as a book about writing. Sometimes Wenmoth speaks confidently, powerfully and truthfully in both the pulpit and his journal, but at other times the voice sounds empty and hollow. He has such little trust in his own preaching that, on occasions, he records the fact that he has preached but "the lesson has already departed my mind" (132) Hobbs sees this as a metaphor for all human creativity, including the art of the novelist and the art of the preacher, often hard work but occasionally effortless, often arid and occasionally productive.

Later in the novel, Wenmoth chooses to preach on Christ's parable of the two builders with which the Sermon on the Mount ends (Matthew 7: 24-7), and he gives readers access to his sermon notes, yet he anticipates neither the storm in his own life nor the storm that hits the church. Deeply saddened that the half empty church in which he preached once brimmed with people who attended in order to be close to heaven, he concludes, "It were an empty sermon which could not have provided them much satisfaction and they must return to their homes still hungry" (109). A storm brews up as he walks away:

> I helped fasten the shutters over the windows of the chapel it seemed we were preparing for a storm like the wise man in the parable but I did not think that this church built on rock served much purpose if no one came to it. We barred the wood door shut closed the chapel tightly no doubt it will lie empty and unused for another week (110).

Faith and vocation put to the test form the themes of this novel. Wenmoth's senses discomfort in the chapels he visits when he feels there is something of him in the stones and wooden pews, but still he itches to be away from them. The frustrations intensify when he is taken to a distress sale for the first time in his life. He cannot think of anything more upsetting than seeing the few meagre possessions of a person fallen on hard times spread out in the hope that someone will bid for them, and then he remembers the contrasting scene at the chapel where harvest produce had been abundantly displayed. Deep dichotomy exists between chapel and world; improvement of humanity's lot achieved by Methodism fails to reach into the economics of the region:

> And this is not the only reason my spirit is quite downcast I cannot avoid the truth of it. I am feeling deep sadness but I tell myself that it should not be indulged in it comes as a temptation tries to deceive our minds to question and doubt (133).

Three aspects of preaching in this novel highlight this temptation to indulge in deep sadness about the failure of religion to affect the way of the world. These aspects nuance the book's depiction of Methodism. First, Wenmoth and his father before him are driven men, self-taught in the practice of preaching. Wenmoth describes his father as having been "called from the mines with no education and no easy life but eloquent in the witness of Christ [because t]here is language come from a heart open to God that the mind cannot know" (45). Neither son nor father finds it easy to walk away from the impulse to share the faith and preach the gospel. Second, their preaching is remorseless and uncompromising. In Wenmoth senior's case, preaching gave way to violence when, once, in what Wenmoth called "a most physical sermon," his father, who often had harsh words for men playing marbles in the street for coins, took a stick to a man sleeping in the sun beside the church (87). Wenmoth thinks himself a lesser Christian because he cannot rise to such actions. Nevertheless, verbal exchanges with non-churchgoing workmen who would pay no heed to his exhortations riled him, and he uses his confessional journal to admit that he has beaten out his anger with iron tools on his anvil and doused them in the water bucket as he cooled the scalding metal. However, there is a third redeeming feature of the preaching in this novel; Wenmoth recognises that the true purpose of all Christian preaching is to encourage believers to be more Christ-like:

> I have been pondering over a lesson in it an image that I will call on for a sermon that we are set the task of imitating our Master and that perhaps we would be better doing less preaching and more in the way of action showing our love of God with our deeds ... The role of the preacher is to illuminate Christ so that others might imitate him and not to shirk action ourselves (53).

Perhaps the Christ-like endurance of suffering that cannot always be alleviated is the primary contemporary and universal theme of *The Short Day Dying*. As Edmund Gordon concluded after interviewing Hobbs, sometimes all we can do is endure and this makes us stronger.[3] Hobbs, preferring not to write about loss of faith, instead writes about a preacher facing a difficult year in his life when faith burns low, who ultimately accepts the freedom to choose for himself and stay away from chapel. In so doing, perhaps Hobbs writes about how faith may endure, away from Methodist chapels and constructs that evolution in his fiction.

Of course, not all fictional Methodists struggle with faith and doubt in such a way that relationships with the local church community are complicated. None of this plotting exists in Unsworth's *The Quality of Mercy*, a sequel to his 1992 Booker Prize-winning *The Sacred Hunger*. The earlier novel recounted an ill-fated and disastrous voyage in which the crew of a slaving ship assisted in the mass execution of its cargo and mutiny against the captain. The voyage ended when the ship was wrecked on the coast of Florida, where the survivors, lacking any hope of early rescue, establish a simple community led by the enlightened ship's doctor. The sequel focuses on two of the survivors, an Irish fiddler called Sullivan and the ship's owner, Erasmus Kemp. The latter pursues a claim for compensation for his loss of income resulting from murders of the jettisoned slaves. *The Quality of Mercy,* set in 1767, concerns the survivors who have been repatriated to Britain and await trial in Newgate prison.

Before the trial begins, however, Sullivan spots an unexpected opportunity to escape and heads north to Durham. He flees, determined to visit the family of his old shipmate, Billy Blair, to whom he had made a promise that, if Blair died, he would do all he could to tell Blair's kin what had befallen him. Late in his writing career (only a year or two before he died), Unsworth returns here to the county of his birth, and this draws attention to the way his literary career differs from those of many of his contemporaries born in the northern counties of England. Whereas other northern writers such as Stan Barstow, John Wain, Sid Chaplin and Alan Sillitoe fixed their gaze on the working-class north, Unsworth moved away from County Durham on winning a scholarship to Oxford and lived for much of his life overseas. Thereafter, characters in Unsworth's novels tended to visit the county of his birth, rather than live there. For instance, the players who take their drama to Durham, in *Morality Play* (1995), are as peripatetic as Unsworth was. Similarly, in *The Quality of Mercy*, an Irishman, Sullivan, merely visits Durham, a county where the Methodist Church retains greater influence than in many other counties of Britain.

As Christopher Potter remarked when reviewing the novel for *The Sunday Times*, "It ought to be obvious who the villains and heroes are in this novel," but the presence of a Methodist among the cast of characters skews the potentially straightforward morality of a tale of ex-slave traders. The Methodist in the novel, Frederick Ashton, fills the role of the lawyer who acts on behalf of the insurance company with the goal of thwarting Kemp's claim for the redeemable insurance value of the ship's cargo. Like many early Methodists, including John Wesley himself, whose last letter was a brief one to William Wilberforce encouraging him in his campaign against slavery, Ashton is a militant abolitionist. However, Unsworth's portrait of the lawyer misdirects readers who find themselves far from sympathetic towards him. Priggish and given to moralising, he tends to address everybody with the rhetoric of high-flown pomposity. Responding, for instance, to an ill-at-ease sailor's claim that they were only following the captain's order when they threw slaves overboard to lighten the ship's load, Ashton loftily says, "But surely there is still a choice to be made? After all, there is a higher law than that of a ship's captain. No man can be obliged to act against his conscience" (73). Taking care not to let his thoughts or feelings show in his face or manner, Ashton, repelled by accounts of life in Florida, sees therein an opportunity to manipulate the legal case:

> The legal case that could be made out of the murder of the slaves and the mutiny that followed had mainly occupied Ashton's thoughts up to now; he had not speculated much about how the survivors had lived afterwards [. . .] He felt immediately repelled, and faintly sickened at the thought of it, black and white fornicating together by turns, displeasing to God and man alike, producing a mixed race. [. . .] On the other hand, the deeper understanding that had come about through this experience of life together in community, if it could be voiced in court, might have an effect on the jury, as showing the absurdity of asserting a right of property in one's fellows on the grounds of race or colour . . . (78).

Opportunistically, Ashton schemes and manipulates facts, appealing to the men's self-interests and telling them that,

> . . . if we can succeed in swaying the jury [that the men later saw the error of their ways] it is more than likely that they will dismiss the capital charges on the grounds that there was no intention to harm, and you will go down in history as heroes of the anti-slavery movement. (79)

But Ashton was thinking,

> And if we fail [...] and you end on the gallows, there is a chance that you will be seen as martyrs, and that is almost as good (79).

Later, Ashton shows that he is willing to use his sister's infatuation with Erasmus Kemp for his personal ends. He suggests that, if Kemp knew that Ashton's plan was what Jane wanted, Kemp might be persuaded to express the view that the mutiny and killing of the captain was justified because it brought an end to the massacre of the slaves. Indeed, Kemp might be persuaded to drop the law suit, but Jane finds her brother's suggestion ugly and unseemly. What he asks of her is little different from what is demanded of slaves; he asks her to put herself in Kemp's hands. But Jane asks in incredulous response, "How can you be so careless of your sister's dignity? How can you be so coarse and selfish?" (172).

Given the anti-slavery stance of many early Methodists, Unsworth's decision to associate Ashton with Methodism is historically appropriate and his depiction is undoubtedly informed by his local knowledge and experience of the denomination in his home town of Wingate. His decision to create this character as one who troubles the story's morality, which, because it is centred on a legal case, would have otherwise been reduced to a simple matter of right or wrong, adds interest to the novel. His decision to make Ashton a man espoused to a worthy cause yet given to unscrupulous behaviour, a man committed to membership of a holiness movement yet showing unbearable moralistic pomposity, troubles the readers' perception of religious faith. Although Ashton is himself untroubled by the matter, readers engaging with this character cannot fail to puzzle over how his deeply-held Methodist beliefs have left some aspects of his character and behaviour untouched.

Many of the Methodist practices in Unsworth's and Carr's novels are reminiscent of independent gospel hall-style Christianity such as that depicted in a 1961 novel by Sid Chaplin. Like Unsworth, Sid Chaplin (1916-1986) was born in a mining village on the Durham coalfield, but, unlike Unsworth, he did not break from his literary roots and has been thought of primarily as a regional novelist. Nevertheless, when Flambard

Press, in 2004, chose to launch its Modern Classics series by reprinting Sid Chaplin's *The Day of the Sardine* and *The Watchers and the Watched*, Michael Brett, in reviewing them in *The Times Literary Supplement,* associated Chaplin with the angrier and slightly younger Angry Young Men such as Alan Sillitoe, Stan Barstow, and John Braine whose novels had already been well-received.[4] These were defiantly northern writers who won nationwide acclaim for their depiction of gritty working class lives. Chaplin formed part of this tradition, a literary descendant of D. H. Lawrence, an older brother of the Angry Young Men, and a literary father to Anthony Burgess's *A Clockwork Orange*. Chaplin's son, Michael, characterised the debate in his father's Newcastle novels as an expression of anxiety about what would happen to old working class values and the moral centre of young people in the northern towns as traditional industry declined and social structures crumbled.[5] For Chaplin, unlike most of his fellow northern writers, this concern resulted from his religious heritage and spiritual experience. As a young man, he served for ten years as a local preacher in the Methodist circuit. He met his wife, Rene, in the Methodist chapel in Kirk Merrington, although, according to their son, she was far from impressed by the sermon. Preaching provided Chaplin with a testing-ground for storytelling; people and their stories fascinated the young preacher more than theology and the Bible. *A Credo*, written in 1964 and reprinted in the posthumous collection of his writing, *In Blackberry Time*, testifies to his growing dissatisfaction with both theology and politics and his increasing fascination with people and their lives. His call to preaching did not last; he said his true call was to writing. Previously, he collected fossils; as a writer, he said he collected people and their stories with an equal passion:

> Theology and philosophy and politics have one thing in common: they attempt to discover or impose a pattern on that very disordered thing we call life. Whatever the pattern is it is never completely satisfying. The human story is a story of individuals. The mere fact that they are born and die shatters the pattern, whatever it is. Perhaps it was this frustration that led me to fiction...
>
> . . .You can tie up the ends in fiction and that is something you can never do in real life. . . As a novelist I don't take up the position of the callow young preacher who said "in the opinion of God and myself . . ." Neither do I take up the position of the man who says "in the opinion of Karl Marx and myself. . .", nor the man who states categorically: "Vanity, all is vanity." No, I prefer to say I am continuously fascinated, obsessed, appalled, amazed and delighted by the infinite variety of human beings, and especially by their capacity for courage, nobility and compassion. (178-9)

Whether or not he is calling his younger self a callow young preacher matters little. Of greatest significance, Chaplin describes a vocational trajectory way from the pulpit to the writing desk where, although he had been a storyteller in the pulpit, he could exercise and express his fascination with people much more successfully than he could within the constraints of northern Methodist chapels. According to his son, Chaplin left Methodism more through circumstance than through dramatic loss of faith. In 1949, a year after the publication of a successful collection of short stories, *The Leaping Lad*, and after ten years as a coal miner, Chaplin was offered a post writing for *Coal*, the magazine of the National Coal Board. Initially, he moved south to take up the post but returned to live in Newcastle in 1957, but by that time the chapel link and his preaching had been lost. Methodism, a strong cohesive social force in northern England, was weaker in the south east, where Chaplin had felt neither social nor inner pressure to attend church. But Chaplin lost neither belief in the worth of humanity nor a sense of a purpose in life, and this drove him to write.[6] Being intrigued by the human condition, passionate about it, and interested in discovering meaning and purpose within it impels some into the pulpit; the same intrigue, passion, and quest kept Chaplin's pen moving.

The Day of the Sardine, the first of Chaplin's Newcastle novels, charts, in first-person colloquial narrative, Arthur Haggerston's uneasy passage into adulthood in a city where soulless manual labour was the only available work and the easiest forms of escape were alcohol and aggression. Within the novel, Arthur's relationships with two women, one older, the other a young Christian, present potential ways he might be saved from waywardness. At the centre of the novel, Arthur records a service in the Golden Bowl Mission, the gospel hall that represents organised religion as a community presence in his neighbourhood. One Saturday night, he has slipped into the hall to avoid two pursuing police officers who suspect he is running away from a fight. Breathlessly pushing his way through a glass-topped swing door, Arthur finds he has stepped into a different world. The swing door, the portal between heaven and earth for him, marks a boundary between the world outside and the security of the world within. When the congregation emotionally lifts the roof with a hymn about Beulah Land, Arthur immediately feels safe as if in Beulah. His brief account of the Saturday evening service reveals an interest in both Dorothy Johnson, the pastor's daughter, and the religiosity expressed in the worship, interests which converge in the prayer Dorothy leads. In her "cornet of a voice" she half-sings a prayer "which went like a poem" and which Arthur feels is for him (165). She prays that God's love will flow through her that it might win for Christ "someone lost" and, after the service, the pastor and his daughter invite Arthur to have a cup of tea. Before he leaves to return home, they invite him to the next day's service.

For Arthur, real religion is secret and magic. The less it is talked about the more chance there is for it to operate; "God wasn't nailed to a cross so that some crazy fool could brag about it" (169). Yet, when he attends the Sunday evening service in the Gospel Hall with his friend Nosey, Pastor Johnson's slick preaching clearly impresses him. From the beginning the service was "full speed ahead." The pastor announced a hymn and "off [the congregation] shot" (187). Attending and participating in the service was like being on an out-of-control fairground ride, scaring Nosey and Arthur. Nosey, feeling threatened, wants to leave only five minutes into the sermon, but there is little about Arthur's description of the preacher's voice to convey the nature of the threat:

> That man had as smooth a voice for talking as his daughter did for singing. It was half-singing anyway, coming out mainly on the toffee range. But sometimes he'd drop to a wind-in-the-wires whisper and let it come forth, resonant (187).

Perhaps Nosey heard the threat within the enticing attempted entrapment contained in the structure of the speech. Arthur, in his narrative, analyses the sermon as am "attack" of four stages—Descriptive, Exhortation, Persuasion and Invitation. Arthur says the first stage is descriptive in that it tells a familiarly biblical metanarrative beginning with security in Eden, spoiled by the serpent, whom the preacher names as the Devil. Centuries of separation follow expulsion, "the treadmill of days" in place of eternity, until the Word made flesh is crucified for our sins (188). The preacher addresses the following "Exhortation" stage to "young people without hope" who run around with easy morals and disregard for God's holy law. He then seeks to persuade them to turn to look at the Crucified, looking into "those wonderful eyes and find the forgiveness you need" (189). The sermon's final stage invites the members of the congregation to bow their heads and lift up their hearts as the preacher prays they will "throw themselves before the seat of Mercy." Arthur perceives himself as a listening man—"Ah'm listenin' all the time" (190)—but he finds that as he attends services during the summer and hears more preaching, he becomes hardened to what is proclaimed. Religion is not going to save his soul from his arid existence. Little, if any, connection exists between the traditionalist form of Christianity represented by the gospel hall and the exciting new world opening out for a young man at the beginning of the 1960s.

At the end of the novel, Arthur expresses a worldview which Michael Chaplin, in interview, described both as humanist and in keeping with the view the author himself reached later in life. Arthur, conscious of sadness and inner dirtiness, listens to a young street preacher, one of Pastor Johnson's prodigies, and dismisses what he hears as gibberish (283). The end evolves for him, melancholy, lonely, and scared, all dressed up and nowhere to go, committed only to "spin (his) own thread" (291), to make his own way in life. An argument can be made that author and character alike make their own narrative and their own sense of life. Evidently, the author, who began adulthood as a Methodist preacher committed to preach nothing other than Methodist doctrine, later finds freedom in his fiction to voice a broader doctrine for a life narrative. The more blinkered enthusiasm of the actual Methodist church and the fictional gospel hall illustrate over-restrictive guides for life. Given that Chaplin's novels have been valued for their documentary quality and what Brett called their "scent of authenticity, drawn from life as it was lived,"[7] they provide evidence that their portrait of the evangelical free church could have been drawn from Chaplin's own experience of Methodists living and working on the Durham coalfield.

Rhidian Brook's debut novel, *The Testimony of Taliesin Jones*, published in 1997 at the beginning of Brook's broadcasting and writing career, features similar gospel hall-style religion from a different region of the United Kingdom. This *Bildungsroman* narrates an eleven-year old boy's search for a true perception of God in a slate-grey Welsh village with the ominously gloomy name of Cwmglum. True perception of God ultimately eludes Taliesin. Looking at, or for, God creates a similar effect as staring at the sun. The brightness forces the watcher to look away and, on looking away, blurred vision results from the continuing presence of "yellow black sun shadows for minutes after" (199). Deep, dazzling darkness both shows and obscures God. Taliesin's struggle to see this black sun begins both in school and the greengrocer's shop where he discovers the nature and purpose of narrative as, puzzled by the absence of Eden in his world atlas, he makes links among a number of stories about apples, including fairy tales, and recognises that in his childhood innocence he feels like Adam before the apple was picked (12). His classmates, compounding his struggle, give him the nickname Worm because of his diminutive stature, he loves reading books, and he "likes to get into the core of things through a slow and persistent questioning" (14). Early in the novel, Taliesin experiences the chapel as a strange place and, although he has not yet questioned the reasons for its existence, (25) readers are sure his childhood development will include spiritual and religious quests. At night, adolescent questions flood into his mind and, despite God having always been "an unseen certainty that he has trusted in," he finds increasing difficulty in imagining God and gives up trying (64). Nevertheless, under the influence of his piano teacher, Billy Evans, he persists in his attempts to pray and conspires with his teacher in conjuring up an image of God as "mover of warts and mountains alike" (87). Having been plagued by warts, when his warts are cured, an entirely unremarkable event experienced by the impressionable boy as both magic and miracle, Taliesin wants the cameras and newsmen of the world to record and report that God has moved his little mountains (106).

Taliesin's spiritual awakening to the shadows of God reaches its twin peaks in an account of a service in the chapel at the top of a hill and in the testimony he gives in school to his fellow pupils, the second giving him an opportunity to internalise and reflect on the first. The author's allusion to the hilltop chapel being a likely refuge in the event of a flood not only associates it specifically with the Ark on which Noah's family and menagerie sailed the great Flood but also accentuates the role of church as a haven safe from what the Victorian hymn writer, Samuel Johnson, called "the surge's angry shock."[8] Taliesin, however, finds no safe haven there. When he attends a service, the large church contains a congregation of no more than thirty, and Taliesin is the only child present. During the singing of hymns, he notices that the preacher's tuneless voice carries to the back of the worship area and an air of menace accentuates Taliesin's observation that all the preacher's movements bore an air of theatricality, which he regards as an attribute of hypocrisy (113). The design of the prayer hassocks includes a palm tree which makes young Taliesin think of an image, derived from William Golding's *The Lord of the Flies,* of "the Flies ... [who] needed God" and who would not have killed Piggy if they had known God (113). The focal point of the service, in which time is measured out by the hymn number rack (116), comes in Preacher Preece's sermon. Preached in a practised, actorly manner and in a well-modulated voice, Preece's sermon about the ingredients which comprise the church makes use of cake ingredients as visual aids and, whilst this seems innocuous, even risible as a sermon subject, Taliesin sustains a threatening element in his account as he observes Preece "looking more like a fox than a fox" (114). Not only has this chapel service filled Taliesin with doubt, but he also tastes the vague bitterness of the preachers' disapproval when they converse at the close of the service. Eventually, Taliesin slips away and, once outside, he "breaks into a run as if he himself were the fox and the preacher a hound from hell" (117).

Later, when Taliesin visits his estranged mother, he attends Christmas Midnight Mass with her new partner. Here he feels quite different. In a church four or five times bigger than the chapel, an air of celebration fills the occasion, and Taliesin feels no compunction to escape.

In his adolescent religious fervour, Taliesin forms a gang called The Believers who share a mission to heal the world, although his misguided attempt to cure William Jones of diabetes endangers Jones's life. After Jones's parents complained to the school about Taliesin's activities, the Headmaster chose to punish him by making him give a Class Assembly, his testimony, which provides the book's title. Compelled to stand before his fellow pupils and state what and why he believes, he expects ridicule; he expects to convince none of his hearers, yet as he begins, the class is hushed. Encouraged, he explains that he has always had a sense of there being a God and that he used to pray without thinking about what he was doing or why. He proceeds to tell them about his piano teacher's ability to perform miracles and claims that anyone in the class could do the same if they had faith. Demands that Taliesin prove this follow, and he finds himself trapped into trying to pray for the regrowth of Hooper's missing finger, severed and lost in a farmyard accident. Of course, no physical change results, but Hooper "yield[s] to something" (188), and, although Hooper had been revealed in the early chapters of the novel as one of the most sceptical of Taliesin's fellow pupils, Taliesin's testimony breaks through Hooper's brittleness; "In exposing just some of his softness to Taliesin, Hooper is opening himself up to possibility. Unbelievably, Hooper wants to believe it is possible" (189). For Taliesin too, glimpses of the bright shadow in which God may be perceived have replaced the gloom of Cwmglum. Not much more can be expected. This tentative sense of God is common to these novels, not only on looking back on a remembered Methodist tradition, but also in the present experience of chapel, whether or not Methodist.

The novels discussed in this chapter show chapel compromised by its zealous righteousness, dogmatic preaching, and resistance to free-thinking society, yet chapel in these fictions can carry within it the potential to discern God as reality and presence. Although generally appreciative of the value of Methodism and its contribution to British society, the overall effect of these novelists' use of the denomination bemoans its diminishing efficacy. Iris Murdoch, J. L. Carr, Barry Unsworth, Sid Chaplin and Rhidian Brook reflect nostalgia for a lost power. They depict Methodist faith as uncompromising in its evangelical zeal and compromised in its out-datedness.

CHAPTER FIVE

O FOR A TRUMPET VOICE ON ALL THE WORLD TO CALL

Many fictional Methodists are preachers. Their sermons reveal their theological views, motivations, and inner personalities. Often novelists find their characters' sermons convenient ways to express and explore religious and ethical viewpoints within their works. As preachers, these characters hold positions of leadership with influence, power, and authority, and face vigorous tests. This chapter concerns these preachers and analyses their preaching, using a methodology which was developed for the benefit of both literary scholars and practising preachers. The fictional preachers within the novels in this study are: Penhale in Joseph Hocking's *Not One in Ten*; Hambly in Quiller-Couch's *Nicky-Nan, Reservist* and John Wesley himself in his *Hetty Wesley*; an unnamed revivalist preacher in Bennett's *Anna of the Five Towns*; John Palehouse in Kaye-Smith's *The Tramping Methodist*; Ellerbeck in Carr's *A Month in the Country*; Pastor Johnson in Chaplin's *The Day of the Sardine*; Hamer Shawcross in Spring's *Fame is the Spur*; and Charles Wenmoth in Hobbs's *The Short Day Dying.*

Something peculiar and particular happens when a novelist writes a sermon. When a novelist includes sermons in a work of fiction, they are out of place, dislocated as essentially oral constructs placed within written texts. They are also hybridised as simultaneously literary, cultural and theological phenomena. Appropriate analysis of such displaced hybrid texts requires resources drawn from several academic disciplines including rhetorical studies, discourse analysis, homiletics and various branches of literary criticism, particularly rhetorical narratology and cognitive poetics. Furthermore, such is the literary and rhetorical complexity of sermons when embedded in novels that fictional sermons can be regarded as a peculiar genre which should be treated with caution. In order to understand Methodist preaching and preachers in British fiction since the dawn of the twentieth century, readers must take account of the peculiarity of the fictional sermon genre.

This is not to say that sermons are unable to hold central, pivotal places in fiction, for, indeed, in many instances they do. Father Mapple's sermon in Melville's *Moby-Dick*, informed by actual Methodist and Puritan preachers, stands as a famous example, and, in Michael Arditti's *Easter*, Blair Ashley's sermon outside a burnt-out church on Easter Day, which mimics John Wesley's actual sermon from a tombstone outside his father's church, bears the heavy thematic and moral load of a crucial climax within the novel.[1] But it is to say that reading a sermon in fiction requires a different inter-active process than that which transpires when hearing it in church or reading it in devotional literature. For instance, a reader's response to Parson Yorick's sermon in Sterne's *Tristram Shandy* creates a reaction quite unlike the response one of Sterne's congregants would make to his actual preaching in church. This differentiation results largely from the displacement of the sermon from its natural discourse community of the people of God at worship to the more playful undefined discourse community of the novel. Nevertheless, the differentiation is not total because the boundaries of the sermon genre, in its natural environment, are soft enough to allow migratory relocation without compromising the reader's capacity to recognise the genre, and still make meaning within and from the text. No loss of readability occurs. Difference, displacement, and uncompromised readability can be assumed when analysing fictional preachers' sermons.

The concept of discourse community holds the sermon together during this process of migration from its oral condition to literary placement. Discourse communities have broadly agreed common goals and shared mechanisms for communication between members which they use to provide information and feedback. They also use at least one literary genre to further their aims. Discourse communities have usually developed a special lexis, or repertoire of vocabulary, in which their members attain at least a threshold level of competence,[2] but, to repeat, any sermon occurring in a novel has migrated from its native discourse community of church to the de-familiarised discourse community of the novel, which comprises its authors, characters, and readers, who may be lacking in the necessary interpretative competence. This de-familiarising migration makes the sermon strange[3] but readers can see it anew.

Bakhtinian theory can help here. In his ground-breaking essay, "The Problem of Speech Genres," Mikhail Bakhtin argued that all utterances comprise thematic content, style, and compositional structure, and he chose to call relatively stable and heterogeneous utterances "speech genres."[4] Genres, he argued, can be either primary or secondary, either simple or complex. Primary genres include letters, diaries, quotidian stories, and speech genres, whereas secondary genres, formed by the combination of primary genres, are more complex. The relationship between primary and secondary genres interested Bakhtin because he saw novels as unique in their insatiable capacity to absorb and digest simple, primary speech genres. Novels are possibly the most complex of secondary speech genres. Furthermore, Bakhtin argued that when a primary genre occurs within a secondary genre, the primary genre changes. His example was a letter within a novel, but sermons in fiction change in a similar way as a result of their migration from orality to literacy. Taking an epochal view of human history, Bakhtin suggested that certain speech genres set the tone for the development of literary language in each epoch; these might include certain types of oral dialogue such as that of the salon. If Bakhtin's historical analysis is correct, it could readily be argued that sermons made major contributions to setting the tone for the development of literary language in eighteenth-century Britain, as Methodism emerged and developed alongside other aspects of Georgian England, and then again in nineteenth-century Britain when the publication of printed sermons outstripped the publication of novels. During these eras, sermonic language certainly inflected other speech genres, and often other literary genres, too.

Bakhtin's concept of heteroglossia, by which he meant that all live utterances are inherently responsive, provides critical assistance. The dynamics of speech make listeners inescapably active participants in any speech utterance. At the same time, speakers also become inescapably respondents. No utterance stands alone; instead, all utterances link in a complexly organised chain of utterances. Consequently, Bakhtin argued, even a single word or phrase can be multiplied and inflected in terms of resonance or response. In his essay, "Discourse in the Novel," Bakhtin had claimed that novels, because they are multiform in style and variform in speech and voice, are distinguished from many other forms of written text by the heteroglossia resulting from the incorporation, within the novel, of other utterances such as authorial speech, narrators' speeches, inserted genres, and characters' speeches.[5] The sermon in fiction is one such sub-genre incorporated within novels which contributes to, and intensifies, their heteroglossia, which means that, like all else in novels, the sermon in fiction is potentially inflected by multiple voicings and meanings. This makes Bakhtin's theory of speech genre and heteroglossia attractive for a critical appreciation of the form and function of sermons in fiction, particularly as Bakhtin's approach does not imply a radical questioning of the role of the author, but privileges the polyphony of the novel in the foreground of its literary critique. Furthermore, it accentuates the social nature of reading. One side benefit of this is that whatever is said in this chapter about fictional preachers and their sermons also applies to actual preachers and their words in their more obvious social setting of the preaching event within an act of worship. Socially constructed guidelines for successful reading govern much literary appreciation, and these assumptions lie behind the discussion of fictional preachers and their sermons in this chapter. (See Appendix).

Regardless of the placing of sermons in fiction, whether thought of as relocation, migration, de-familiarisation or translation, when the discourse communities have overlapping characteristics, when the direction of transfer is from the more rhetorically-accessible to the less rhetorically-accessible and when there is a perceived rationale for communicative behaviour within the genres (for instance, when there is a community of believers hearing the preaching), the boundaries between them can be soft enough to permit translation. Skills in reading within one genre may then be transferred to reading within another, so long as the reader acknowledges the transfer. Despite the reading public's decreasing access to actual preaching, the claim that sufficient overlap exists between the sermon-genre and the sub-genre of sermon-in-fiction to permit accessibility of both genres to their respective discourse communities still stands. Whatever a sermon in fiction teaches, an actual sermon can also teach, and *vice versa*.

When making a critique of a fictional sermon, four aspects need to be considered—its audiences, its speaker, its argument and its language.[6] Analysis of the preaching in the novels studied in this book begins with the two classics *Adam Bede* and *Anna of the Five Towns*. Following these classics, analysis of the preaching in twentieth- and twenty-first-century novels will reveal contrasting styles—foundational preaching, troubled preaching, and the capacity for a crossover from preaching to political oratory—each of which will be discussed below.

First, on the strength of her single sermon in the second chapter of *Adam Bede*, Dinah Morris has arguably become the best known Methodist preacher in English fiction. Modelled on George Eliot's aunt, Dinah identifies herself with John Wesley. The sermon ends with an evangelical call to repentance. It begins both with allusions to Jesus among the teachers in the Temple, as recounted in Luke's Gospel, announcing good news for the poor and with Dinah's memories of being taken to hear John Wesley preach on the same text. The author directly quotes Dinah's sermon in all but two of its sections. In the first, after claiming that humankind is in sad want of good news, Eliot summarises a section of unspecified length, although the entire sermon lasted at least an hour:

"Then Dinah told how the good news had been brought, and how the mind of God towards the poor had been made manifest in the life of Jesus, dwelling on its lowliness and its acts of mercy" (70). This summary, which embodies the conventions of Methodist Christology and mission, suggests to the critic that a potential starting point for a critical appraisal might be the sermon's argument.[7]

Dinah's formulaic manner of commencing the sermon with a prayer establishes her as a virtuous person; she bows her head, closes her eyes and continues in the same moderate tone to pray as if addressing someone standing next to her. Thus, she establishes the appearance of an intimate relationship with Jesus, whom she addresses in the prayer as "Saviour of Sinners," without distancing herself from her audience to whom she appears humble. Nevertheless, the prayer contains a clear indication to the audience that she has a life-changing message to which they would do well to listen. The sermon will end equally formulaically with an invitation "to take [the] blessedness [that] is offered to you" (76), adding a verse of one of Charles Wesley's hymns, effectively rooting her preaching firmly in the Methodist tradition:

> Its streams the whole creation reach,
> so plenteous is the store,
> enough for all, enough for each,
> enough for evermore.

The words and works of both Wesley brothers and the Bible are the only intentional intertexts of the sermon, characteristic of Methodist preaching of that era, as well as of Wesley's own preaching. His published sermons, used to define orthodox Methodist doctrine among his preachers of later generations, allude to almost nothing other than the Bible. So closely does Dinah's sermon adhere to classical Methodist preaching that Eliot felt a need to defend herself against the charge of merely copying her character's words from life: "They were written," she wrote in a letter, "with hot tears, as they surged up in my own mind!"[8]

The narratival direction of Dinah's sermon moves from Jesus in the Temple to her memory of Wesley in the open air, both of whom preached on the Old Testament prophet Isaiah's pronouncement of God's mission of good news to the poor. Wesley was an old man by the time Dinah heard him, but significantly, Jesus' quotation of Isaiah was the text which Wesley used the first time he broke free from the walls of a church and preached outdoors. Eliot, thus, establishes Dinah at the centre of the Methodist preaching tradition; her gender does not push her to the margins at this stage of the novel. From her memory of Wesley preaching, Dinah moves to self-denigration as well as self-identification with her audience's poverty:

> Why, you and me, dear friends, are poor. We have been brought up in poor cottages, and been reared on oat-cake and lived coarse: and we haven't been to school much, nor read books, and we don't know much about anything but what happens just around us. We are just the sort of people that want to hear good news (69).

Dinah's adopted role as peer of the audience merges with the humble and devout persona, established at the beginning, to win the attention of the crowd gathered at the village green. Having previously asked whether the villagers would not love such a man as Jesus if they saw him (70), Dinah dramatically invokes the very presence of Jesus. With her eyes fixed on a point directly above the people's heads, she turns to the right and exclaims, "See! See where our blessed Lord stands and weeps. . . " (74). There follows a powerful passage in a similar vein, in which Dinah evokes an image of Christ standing before them pleading with them that what he suffered, he did for them: "All this he bore for you. . . I see his wounded body and his look of love." (74). She dares them to look away. Here, a strong element of theatricality has entered the preaching. From this general admonition not to close their ears to Jesus' plea, Dinah turns her individual attention to Bess Cranage. With fear of "everlasting fire", Dinah terrorises Bess who, unable to bear it any longer, sobs aloud, then, in the second short section of reported speech, Eliot informs readers that "Dinah began to tell of the joys that were in store for the penitent, and to describe in her simple way the divine peace and love with which the soul of the believer is filled" (75). The sermon draws towards its finale as Dinah, in a few minutes of personal testimony, attests to knowing this blessedness. She adopts once again the tone of identification with the audience as she says, "Because I know [this blessedness], I want you to have it too. I am poor, like you: I have to get my living with my hands, but no lord or lady can be so happy as me, if they haven't got the love of God in their souls." (76). Dinah then brings her sermon to a conclusion with her final appeal and the verse of Wesley's hymn.

Comparisons between Dinah's preaching and a theatrical performance might have already occurred to the novel's readers. Preaching, in that it tells a single narrative, is more like drama than a music hall act; the preacher "acts" her part and an audience engages with the event.[9] Indeed, evidence establishes that early Methodist preachers were commonly regarded as theatrical, which opened the way for some biting satires mocking the hypocrisy of outspoken men like George Whitefield, who objected to theatre, but readily employed theatrical gestures and vocal techniques in their preaching.[10] Within *Adam Bede,* however, the stranger on horseback watches and listens to Dinah's sermon "as if it had been the development of a drama" without any hint of satire or criticism (76). Common ground shared by preaching and theatre brings into question the nature of the space used in the preaching event; how formal is the event? Using terms Bakhtin employed, the preaching act may be described as either centrifugal, in that it is as formal as a play performed under a proscenium arch, or centripetal, in that it is more informal and comparable to the more flexible theatrical experience of a play in an intimate theatre in the round.[11] In the case of Dinah's preaching event, whilst the outdoor village green location lends an air of flexibility in which individual audience members can stand on the fringes and come and go without interrupting proceedings, the event's organisers, local Methodists, cannot resist their innate need to establish a church-like place on the green. Eliot carefully sets the scene. Unusually, the green lies at the extremity of Hayslope where the road branches in two directions, up the hill towards the church and down towards the valley, thus emphasising that Dinah preaches, not only in the open air, but on the edge of civilisation. Any further from the village, she would be in wild countryside. Within this natural and random environment, local Methodists place benches and set up a cart to be used as a pulpit. These simple schemata of church establish for the reader the notion that an event with elements of formality will occur in this open, flexible and natural place. Pews for the people and a pulpit for the preacher provide the basic furniture of church.

The preacher's persona makes or breaks the act of preaching. Eliot carefully introduces Dinah as a local stranger. She comes from a village thirty miles away, near enough to be known by reputation, but far enough away not to be known intimately. She can retain both an air of familiarity and a respected distance. The horseback stranger knows of only two types of Methodist—the bilious and the ecstatic (66)—and Dinah is neither of these. She enjoys an absence of self-consciousness. Indeed, Eliot adopts a *via negativa* approach to her description of Dinah, referring more to personal attributes that are absent in Dinah and less to what can be ascribed to her personality. This effectively depicts her as an innocent outsider, untainted by whatever has previously rendered other Methodist preachers suspect to Hayslope villagers.

Eliot cannot overlook Dinah's gender when establishing her status as a preacher. Wiry Ben, one of the villagers, is excited by the prospect of hearing Dinah preach, although her appearance interests him more than the sound of her clear voice: "She's a pleasant-looked 'un," he says (65), and he suspects that he is more likely to be converted by a pretty woman than an ugly man. Is Eliot implying that preachers like Dinah can be more persuasive as a result of their beauty or is she implying that her divine work can be compromised by her womanly charms and the impious motives of male hearers? It could go either way. In the event, Dinah behaves demurely as she preaches; part of her performance presents her as a quiet, composed and calm woman of God.

Dinah's sermon has more audiences than Dinah could have ever imagined. The actual intra-textual audience—the sermon's hearers within the novel—is itself diverse. Yet, to it can be added at least three more audiences: Dinah's implied audience within the text, Eliot's intended readership which forms an extra-textual actual audience, and her actual, but unintentional, readership since the novel's original publication which forms an extra-textual implied audience.[12] Within the novel itself, Dinah's audience comprises a series of receding circles. At the centre, around Dinah as she stands under the maple tree, is a "knot of Methodists" (61), an expectant audience in Quaker-like dress. Everyone else present at the event takes care not to join this tiny group; most of the men were gathered near the blacksmith's shop where they could see and hear what was going on but not so near as to be regarded as interested in joining in; the women, who were more curious than their men folk, had edged forward to gather on the edge of the green. The horse-rider passing through overlooks the entire scene. Once the sermon gets underway, Eliot, following Dinah's example, focuses on several individuals so readers can learn their reaction to Dinah's sermon: Feyther Teft was too deaf to hear and Wiry Ben wished he hadn't heard. Wiry Ben worried that he was being drawn into the sermon and would be thereafter haunted by it, especially after he saw Sandy Jim wipe tears from his eyes. The all-seeing and authoritative narrator explains that what moved Sandy Jim was his resolution to go to the Holly Bush less often (73). Bess Cranage's reactions, told in the most detail, trace the sermon's effects on her. She listens intently to Dinah, her eyes fill with tears, her lips grow pale, she feels great terror within, and she throws her earrings to the ground. Despite their intention not to be drawn in, their initial curiosity, of varying degrees, exposed several of the villagers to the possibility of persuasion. The famous, probably apocryphal, tale contrasting two Greek orators comes to mind. Unlike the speaker who merely inspired admiration for his oratory, Dinah compares favourably with the more effective other who also inspired his hearers to march; Dinah's preaching moved at least some of the villagers to belief and action.[13]

All credit should be given to Dinah. The stranger on horseback, through whose eyes Eliot sees the event and whose perspective filters the sermon, notes that Dinah's entrancing voice and quiet conviction unequivocally communicate the truth of her message. He does not doubt that her calmness will entrance her hearers, and he soon sees her ability to hold their attention. He observes that there was no change of attitude or gesture as she preached; rather, her speech was made effective simply by the inflections of her voice (71). Nevertheless, Eliot's telling of the sermon indicates Dinah's skilful use of pauses and accelerations as she spoke. Dinah mimicked no one, despite her self-claimed identification with John Wesley: "She was not preaching as she heard others preach, but speaking directly from her own emotions, and under the inspiration of her own simple faith" (72). Greater integrity can be expected of no preacher. Dinah Morris impresses by her "sincere unpremeditated eloquence" (76).

This discussion of Dinah Morris's sermon, alone, could ably serve as an introduction to discussions of Methodist sermons in later novels but, in the cause of completeness, giving attention to the revivalist sermon on Arnold Bennett's *Anna of the Five Towns* will form an interesting contrast. Whereas Dinah's sermon receives appreciative treatment both within *Adam Bede* and amongst its readers, neither Bennett nor his readers share the approval given by some in the revivalist's congregation to his sermon.

Anna of the Five Towns is the first of Bennett's novels to use the Potteries as its setting, and, in the sermon given by the guest evangelist at the local Methodist church, his disapproval of the control Methodism held over the local population becomes obvious. Anna, who arrives late, must go to the gallery for a seat as the seat in the gallery grants a panoramic overview of proceedings. She can look over the scene as easily as the horseback rider could in *Adam Bede*. Most of the floor space in Methodist churches of the time was filled with pews facing a central raised pulpit, often wide enough for more than one occupant. Behind the pulpit, and in front of the organ pipes, tiered ranks of pews were set for the choir, who faced the congregation in performance mode. The gallery in which Anna sat would typically form a 'U' along the sides and rear of the church, or in smaller churches fill the rear only. Often the only place visible to every seat in every pew was the pulpit. These buildings were, above all else, preaching halls and were often referred to as town-hall style churches. When Anna takes her place in the gallery, the foreboding presence of the stout pale-faced Superintendent Minister standing impassively looking at the assembly with cold grey eyes dominates the scene from his vast mahogany pulpit. Alongside him is the evangelist. She believes they watch her disapprovingly.

The revivalist sermon is particularly interesting for Bennett's awareness of audience. As Anna arrives, she sees and feels the air of expectation among the gathered people in the crowded chapel, excited, eager and impressed. They sang the opening hymn with unprecedented vigour and sincerity; the choir, "usually perfunctory, seemed to share the general fervour" (66). The preacher brings low his actual intra-textual audience, as they respond to his preaching with a sense of shame and humility; everyone, except the organist who was busy finding the next hymn in his tune-book, felt bitterly ashamed as if caught in the very act of sin (67). As the preacher continued, the congregation broke out into a catalogue of sighs, groans, blessings and Amens, which led Anna to assume that their level of expectation was so high they were sure they would not be disappointed. Already, though, readers know that both Anna and the organist are distracted and distanced from the others. She notices others who are inattentive—a glum youth and Henry Mynors, who was whispering to the organist from his place in the orchestra. The inattention does not last. Both the youth and Mynors leave their places to go into the enquiry room where counsellors will pray with them. On seeing them go, Anna is quite suddenly overcome. Previously moved to sorrow and anger because she was beginning to feel penitent (69),

> Anna was now in the profoundest misery. The weight of her sins, of her ingratitude to God, lay on her like a physical and intolerable load, and she lost all feeling of shame, as a sea-sick voyager loses shame after an hour of nausea. She knew then that she could no longer go on living as aforetime. ... She heaped up all the wickedness of a lifetime, hysterically augmented it, and found a horrid pleasure in the exaggeration. Her virtuous acts shrank into nothingness (70).

Certain value-laden expressions within this report expose Bennett's awareness of an audience beyond that in the chapel—an extra-textual audience comprising the readers for whom Bennett writes. He speaks to readers over the heads of the preacher and his hearers. Bennett's disapproval of Methodism as an organisation for gloomy, forbidding and sombre people is compounded here by his representation of the congregation's exaggerated fervour and disingenuous responses to the preaching. Readers suspect that Anna's response, described as hysterical, is false; why else would she enjoy the exaggeration? Bennett leads his extra-textual audience to see through the rally's apparent success of "a superb record" of seventy saved souls (95) as being due to the fragility of the congregation's response to a manipulative preacher. Detached observers will ask how lasting the penitence of the respondents will be when the preacher is a self-proclaimed mountebank and the audience's sense of sinfulness is exaggerated beyond truthfulness.

Reminiscent of Bennett's dismay that doom-laden posters outside churches were not more encouraging, the revivalist's first words, after a solemn and dreadful pause, are "Behold us, O dread God, suppliants for thy mercy. . ." (67). His address is neither to a loving God nor an eternal God, not even to a merciful or almighty God. Rather, his words place people in dread of God, pleading for mercy. Moreover, when he invites people to join him in further prayer after a hymn, his invitation is, "Let us engage in private prayer. Let us drive the devil out of this chapel" (69). Again, his words assume the presence of wickedness in the assembly; there is little acknowledgement, if any, of goodness among the people there. His extraordinary histrionic gift enables the preacher to communicate to his human audience a sense that God is a second audience alongside them (67). Of course, liturgically speaking, sermons are humbly offered to God along with all else that takes place in the Sunday service. But that is not what Bennett suggests here. Rather, the revivalist's carefully calculated effects allow him to dominate his human audience while impressing on his human hearers a sense that his words are acceptable to God. He draws attention to himself without pointing away from his performance towards God. His fiery, inquisitive eyes are all-seeing and intensely burning (66), and he is capable not only of silencing, but also of humbling and shaming his congregation with a hand gesture. His rich, sharp, and decisive voice subdues their eager anticipation and holds their attention, but he is a charlatan who knows he uses unscrupulous tactics to achieve his own ends. The church porch carried a notice indicating that cabinet photographs of the revivalist, ever one to benefit personally from his vocation, can be purchased at a shilling each. When inviting congregants to put sixpence each in the offering, he employs what Bennett calls "ferocious sarcasm." If any among them resent a collection, they can keep their miserable sixpences and get six-pennyworth of miserable enjoyment out of them elsewhere (69). No politness phenomena occur here, as in most suasory speeches, where speakers defuse potentially face threatening acts by using politeness markers.[14] This evangelist is, to use colloquial terms, in your face.

Remarkably, some twenty-first century Methodists can continue to be fond of Arnold Bennett despite the jibes he lobs at Methodists, because they see in his Potteries-based novels a community which is held together by the close ties of the movement. Some can blinker their eyes from his fierce criticism of a controlling organisation and still enjoy his depiction of the community-shaping, socially-cohesive Church they remember. Most, however, feel the force of Bennett's disapproval.

Bennett's charlatan revivalist is as far removed from Dinah Morris as it is possible to be. Sheila Kaye-Smith's *The Tramping Methodist* contains a similar, but less extreme, contrast of preaching styles, those of the narrator, Humphrey Lyte, and his unofficial mentor, John Palehouse. In this novel, the eponymous tramping Methodist is its narratival voice and he, Humphrey Lyte, reports his own preaching in the village of Rolvenden. The sleepy villagers there, too indolent to interrupt or laugh, allow young Lyte to gain confidence as he speaks. In the manner of John Wesley, who was well-schooled in the Church Fathers and often cited them, Lyte had chosen some words of Thomas à Kempis for his text. He reports that for more than an hour he preached of the broken heart and of the bleeding Hand which alone can bind it (his capitalisation). When he ends, a voice at his elbow cries out, "Well done!" Such a response, like a bravo! after the tenor's aria, praises a performance, but it does not signify effective preaching, for preaching's aim is more than to win the audience's admiration. Its productive task moves its members either to adopt certain beliefs or to take action. The voice belongs to John Palehouse.

Soon after this sermon, Palehouse preaches in the village of Benenden. In contrast with Palehouse's gentle "Well done!" to Lyte's preaching, Lyte is struck dumb by Palehouse's eloquence. When Palehouse preaches in the open air, Kaye-Smith uses to great effect the naturalistic backdrop; the wind strengthens the preacher, the birds that cleave the blue air over the tree-tops add swiftness to his words, and the thunder that rumbles behind the hills gives them fierceness (118). Palehouse is one with God's creation as he speaks, and the clouds part over his head so that the sun kisses his hair, as if in benediction, as he kneels to pray (134). Even so, Lyte notices that Palehouse is a different man when he preaches; he has two personalities. "Your life and your gospel ill agree," he accuses (119), to which Palehouse claims that his preaching is given to him from God. He knows he is a milder man away from the pulpit, but he sees this as no weakness. In his desire to encourage people to flee from the wrath that is to come—Wesley's basis for evangelical conversion—he allows himself to be taken over by God to become more fierce and zealous in his speech.

Lyte describes Palehouse's sermons as stern, rugged, and ruthless. His subject matter is death, hell and judgement, and the driving force of his preaching is fear of hell. A well-educated man, Palehouse debases his language when he preaches, borrowing the rough, ill-chosen uncultured speech of his rural audiences so that they relate to what he says. Usually, Lyte notes, Palehouse's conversation is peppered with what he calls

Biblical phraseology; for instance, "preaching" with Palehouse is "prophesying" and going before someone is "preventing" that person (109). This mixture of native speech and biblical language presents Palehouse as a preacher who accommodates his hearers.

The chief contrast between the mentor and his student comes when Lyte's confidence wavers. Where Palehouse had spoken of death and judgement, Lyte had spoken of Christ and eternal life; where Palehouse had threatened with the fear of hell, Lyte had enticed with the hope of heaven; where Palehouse dwelt on Old Testament scenes and characters, Lyte chiefly spoke of the New; and where Palehouse spoke of God as Jehovah, mighty and to be feared, Lyte preached of God as the loving and beloved Father (118). The greatest difference, however, comes from the responses of hearers. When Lyte preached, the most favourable response he had was "stolid, unmoved faces" but sometimes he was victim of open jeering. When Palehouse preached, no one jeered. Men were moved and even excited. Tears coursed down women's cheeks. Palehouse's sermons were greeted with the silence of bated breath.

Nevertheless, the reception in the village of Biddenden was an exception. Ignoring the local curate's warning that he did not want any of their "demned ranting in [his] parish" (133), Palehouse had only just begun to preach when the crowd's jeering turned to violence as villagers picked up stones and threw them. Palehouse was silenced, but this did not stop the angry crowd. They continued until he was unconscious. The scene at the end, with Palehouse lying with his face buried in the thyme and blood trickling from his head, shoulders, arms and sides, made Lyte think of St. Stephen, except that unlike the first Christian martyr, Palehouse was silent (135). Unlike Arnold Bennett, great critic of Methodism, Kaye-Smith expresses approval for neither preacher over the other. She describes the contrast between Humphrey Lyte and his mentor through Lyte's narrative without expressing authorial judgement.

In Sir Arthur Quiller-Couch's *Hetty Wesley* the sermons belong to the era of the foundations of Methodist preaching and readers are presented with a fictionalised version of Wesley as a preacher. Two instances of John Wesley's preaching occur in the novel. The first occurs shortly after Wesley has written to his brother, Samuel, that leisure and he had taken leave of each other because he was resolved to be busy as long as he lived. Here Quiller-Couch gives an account of Wesley preaching a difficult sermon at Wroote Church, while still a curate to his father. The other is an account of one of the eight occasions Wesley preached while standing on his father's tomb, after being barred from preaching in his late father's church.

The difficult circumstances of the first of these sermons raise the intriguing question of preacher status and self-consciousness.[15] The fifteenth chapter of *Hetty Welsey* begins with a quotation from the Gospels which Wesley seems to be thinking of using as the text of a sermon which will bring into the open a family dispute. Wesley plans to use the sermon to reproach his father publicly for judging Hetty unfairly. At first, Wesley struggles to plan the sermon. He lays down the Bible and leans against the tree he is sitting under with his eyes half closed. Unlike other sermons that arrange themselves quite neatly and rapidly, Wesley's thoughts are too random and confused to form a coherent sermon. Only after conversation with his sister, Molly, about his quandary does the sermon flow from his pen. Then returning to his bedroom, Wesley completed the sermon's script in two hours. In those days, curate's sermons were usually approved by their vicars and rectors before preaching, so the sermon was duly sent to his father. Although it criticised his father's behaviour, it was returned unmarked, ready for preaching.

What can be assumed, then, about the fictional Wesley's consciousness as a preacher? Evidently, he identified a role for testimony within preaching; the preacher not only stood in the pulpit, but also brought into it his personality, beliefs, and life-story, which informed the contents of the sermon. This moves the sermon from a scholarly discourse to a preaching act. In the case of the sermon in *Hetty Wesley*, testimony will include testifying against his father (192). The preacher exposes himself and his family, before God and the general public, as people who have sinned against Christ's injunction to judge not. The fictional Wesley has duties under Christ to all souls in his care (193). Thus, in his sermon, he expresses the divine will, but not as his congregation's superior. Readers might ask what in this sermon indicates that the preacher believes he is speaking on behalf of God, whether the focus is on the teller or on what the teller points towards. The fictional Wesley does both. By pointing to his own family, he shows himself to be subject to God's commands, as are his hearers. By his own words, he risks compromising his own reputation and positions himself as one in need of God's mercy as they are.

The other aspect of this sermon especially worthy of attention is its argument. That Wesley senior returned it unmarked implies its strength; he accepted its argument. In addition, the novel gives readers two tentative titles for the sermon, a quoted section, an indication of the fictional Wesley's performance frames[16] and the response the sermon evokes. The titles the fictional Wesley considers are "Universal Charity" or "The Charity due to wicked persons." One hopes the former is eventually chosen as the latter merely prolongs the judgemental attitude the sermon is meant to counteract. The quoted section references several biblical passages: Christ's cleansing of the Temple, Christ's cursing of the fig tree, Christ's denunciation of the Pharisees and enjoyment of the company of sinners, the rejoicing in heaven over the one who repents, and the psalmist's affirmation that "a broken and contrite heart, O God, thou wilt not despise." Such extensive use of the Bible in no more than one paragraph of a sermon is in keeping with the actual Wesley's own practice.[17] The directly quoted section concludes:

> Yet we in this parish have despised [a broken and contrite heart]. With sorrow I admit before you that in the household to which you would reasonably look for example and guidance, it has been despised. What then? Are we wiser than Christ, or more absolute? (195).

Then the preacher pauses. This performance frame, which concludes a powerful section, is bolstered by the narrator's description of the fictional Wesley looking straight down into the rectory pew, and once or twice involuntarily seeking the gaze of its occupants (194). This is nothing other than controlled confident preaching in difficult circumstances, conveying to the reader that the preacher had a strong sense of rectitude. His mother, Susannah, sat stiff and upright with her eyes bent to the ground; Charles and Molly alone looked up; Emilia and Patty frowned and Kezzy fidgeted with her prayer-book. The chapter concludes with the telling comment: "Not a word was said of the sermon," contrary to the usual pattern of conversation in which sermons were dissected over lunch (195). Overall, Quiller-Couch's account of this sermon presents the fictional Wesley as a prophet in his own house.

The other sermon in the novel gives an account of one of the most famous of John Wesley's sermons, one when, excluded from the church in Epworth, he made himself more vile, clambered onto his father's tomb and preached in the open air. Quiller-Couch chooses to convey this sermon to the reader through the eyes of a fictional commentator, John Whitelamb[18] who had been Hetty's first love. Seven years have passed since the ill-fated relationship had ended, and Whitelamb, appearing prematurely aged, now stands apart from the crowd where, between fear and hope of being recognised, he can overlook the scene and hear the sermon. He feels worthy of contempt and is conscious that, in the intervening years, the Wesley family had entirely neglected him and left him with "his miserable doubts" (268). They had cast him off. Can Quiller-Couch's readers expect, therefore, an impartial account of the sermon? Will Whitelamb's angle of telling be coloured by his experience, because the way he had been treated by the Wesley family might inflect his reception of the sermon and compromise the integrity of the preacher? Wesley's voice reached Whitelamb "as one rending the sepulchre", piercing his whole being so that it "unlock[ed] old wells of tears" (268). The tree under which Whitelamb stood, and from which he enjoyed a clear view of proceedings, is a sycamore, reminiscent of the scene in Luke's Gospel where Zacchaeus, also a neglected soul, climbs a sycamore so that he may have a clear view of Jesus as he passed by. The indirect intertextual association of Whitelamb with Zacchaeus casts Whitelamb in his worn-out clerical black gown as an outcast whose heart the preacher, Wesley, might unexpectedly open.[19] After the event, Whitelamb is moved to dare to write to Wesley offering to assist him in whatever way Wesley chooses—"Glad I should be that you would make use of me"—but his letter receives only a brief reply which implies it has been only cursorily read (270).

As Whitelamb looks around during Wesley's sermon, he sees Romley, the curate who had denied Wesley permission to preach in his late father's old church. Clearly, Whitelamb does not approve of Romley's behaviour, noting that Romley watched "with a loose-lipped sneer; too weak to conquer his own curiosity, far too weak to assert his authority and attempt to clear the churchyard of that 'enthusiasm' which he had denounced in his most florid style last Sunday, within the church" (268). Clearly, Whitelamb, despite just cause for ill feeling, still has some sympathy for his old friend. He hears something that reminds him of Wesley senior in John Wesley's sermon, yet, as he leaves the scene once the sermon is over, he comes away intellectually unconvinced while still marvelling at the power he had witnessed. Such was the emotional effect of Wesley's preaching that Whitelamb's heart is bursting with love. Little textual evidence exists within *Hetty Wesley* that the fictional Wesley was in any way troubled either by Whitelamb's presence at the back of the crowd or by guilt that his family may have treated Whitelamb unjustly. Given that his first sermon had been prompted by his conviction that Hetty had been treated unfairly, the absence of a similar conviction about her lover now is ironic. The fictional Wesley seems to have outgrown his troubles.

Other fictional Methodist preachers in twentieth- and twenty-first century novels are more conscience ridden. Many are troubled or troubling. The next section considers three.

The first of these is Ellerbeck, more troubling than troubled, in J. L. Carr's *A Month in the Country*. The novelist's protagonist, Tom Birkin, whose upbringing had been decidedly non-religious with his father's choosing to praise his Maker while fishing from the riverbank rather than in church, and who had become an unbeliever when he was seventeen or eighteen, finds himself thrown into the deep end of Wesleyan Methodism on his month away from home because he is expected to attend chapel with his host, Ellerbeck. Like most in the vicinity, Ellerbeck had left school after only an elementary education but had become a local preacher in his late teens. He maintains his preaching ministry by depending on mimicking earlier models. His father had been a passionately violent and irrational man, and, although Ellerbeck was mild-mannered and self-contained in comparison, he became his father when he entered the pulpit. He announced hymns and led prayers, or, as the non-believer Birkin describes prayer, "tediously supplicatory obeisance at [an] oriental despot's skirts" (43), in a mild and acceptable manner, but, once launched on the waves and billows of his sermon, he roared and bellowed like a madman, banging his fist on the podium in an alarming manner, as his father had done. Although making some allowance for Birkin's point of view when reporting this service, Ellerbeck's lack of training and his reliance on an out-dated model that neither suits his personality nor allows for changes of expectation as time passes poses a more troubling aspect.

Alarmingly for any reader who cares about preaching, there is a second sermon in Carr's novel, for Birkin himself is persuaded to stand in for Ellerbeck. The Superintendent Minister has planned Ellerbeck for a service in a tiny rural chapel without allowing sufficient travel time from his previous appointment, so Birkin helps out. In his reminiscence of the occasion, Birkin tells of a congregation comprising an organist, two adults and two children, none of whom were deceived by the stumbling extemporary prayer Birkin led near the beginning of the service. After singing another hymn, Birkin resolves to abandon his "awful impersonation" of a preacher and, more forcefully than he intended, he announced, "Look here ... I'm just filling in and, as I've not preached before and certainly shan't again, I'm going to tell you what I'm doing in Oxgodby and, if you want to leave or nod-off [sic], that's alright by me" (54). Birkin tells the novel's readers nothing of what he said in the address, though it is safe to surmise that it was more of a talk than a sermon. He held no belief in what he was doing when leading the congregation in worship. The lack of guidance offered to this young man as he occupied this position of authority must have troubled him, as would trouble anyone if what happened to the fictional Birkin, based on real life experience, continued in the church of the present day.

Wenmoth in Peter Hobbs's *The Short Day Dying* is another troubled preacher. One, albeit short, chapter of this novel comprises Wenmoth's notes for a sermon on Jesus' parable of the two builders. One of Hobbs's interests in writing this novel was to explore the dichotomy between narratives about the self and the reality that does not quite match self-perceptions. The bare sermon notes, in the twenty-second chapter of the novel, expose this dichotomy within Wenmoth at his most vulnerable. The sermon was to be preached at Crafthole but, in the form presented in the novel, the sermon is taken from this context and given an implied context of Wenmoth's anxieties and difficulties as a preacher. From Jesus' parable, which the first Gospel places as the conclusion to the Sermon on the Mount, Wenmoth chooses to focus on the building with poor foundations, and he took as his text, "And it fell and great was the fall of it," rather than taking positive encouragement from the building that stood firm. The barebones of this sermon, naked on the page, expose Wenmoth's failure to learn the lessons he himself teaches—to be sure of firm foundations, to counter weariness by listening for God's encouraging word, and to resist fearfulness when the storm blows hard and the floods surge. When Wenmoth records in his journal what he experienced when he preached from these notes at Crafthole, he expresses disappointment that the attendance is as low as it is—just two others apart from him. He feels sadness that the chapel that was raised with such hope now attracts so few faithful people: "Seems there is little faith remaining" (109). He records dismay that, instead of feeling the voice of God filling him, he laboriously dragged words from the Bible and turned them on his own tongue. Wenmoth records no sense of being God's mouthpiece as a preacher, but feels alone in the pulpit working hard to deliver an "empty sermon" which sent members of the congregation back to their home hungry. This is bleak.

A later journal entry records a service in the village chapel of Forder, but Wenmoth is unable to remember the lesson and he reports feeling uncomfortable in churches where he once felt at home (132). Unable to find his own voice, unable to feel comfortable in the pulpit, and unable to be himself as a preacher, he resorts to preaching like his father and grandfather. This produces nothing but feelings of despondency, deep sadness and depression in his disappointment that he feels none of God's grace or glory. He realises, then, that the stony ground of Jesus' parable of the sower and the seed is his own heart.

Because all of Wenmoth's preparation for preaching, actual preaching and personal reaction to the experience of preaching, is communicated to the novel's readers through Wenmoth's journal, Hobbs privileges his readers with Wenmoth's inner turmoil as a man wrestling with vocation. Apart from Wenmoth's own awareness of the effect this has on his hearers, such as feeling the sermon he preached at Crafthole was empty, readers do not know whether or not congregations were voting with their feet and staying away when Wenmoth's appearance was planned. No evidence indicates either way. Actual preachers know that how they feel about a sermon they have preached is an unsure guide to its effectiveness; sermons that feel perfunctory or empty to the preacher can sometimes be well-received. The preacher is not always the best judge of the sermon.

The third troubled preacher is Quiller-Couch's character, Hambly, who lived and worked through the troubling times of the First World War. In *Nicky-Nan, Reservist*, Hambly preaches two sermons amidst his personal disillusionment with the Church and his own ministry within it. Miss Polsue's response to one is "Have you ever heard a feebler or more idiotic sermon?" Miss Oliver responds to the other, "Silly old rigmarole!" Is the assessment of either of these women fair? Four facts from the text suggest they are not: first, Miss Polsue, seemingly missing the main thrust of the first sermon, focuses on a secondary point Hambly made about Sabbath observance, second, missing the thrust of the second sermon, she focuses on the notion that God has a purpose for typhoid fever (the direct opposite of what Hambly said), third, the two women worry about whether Hambly is a smoker and, fourth, they determine that the circuit should invite a married man next time. These ill-informed comments combine to put the sagacity of their judgement into question.

Quiller-Couch reports much of both sermons in direct speech as quoted monologue.[20] Reading the preacher's quoted words makes possible an assessment of the reasoning and argument of his speech. After a prayer, for which a simple hand gesture had bidden all to kneel, Hambly begins his sermon with a creaking voice that nevertheless impressed many with its tone of sincerity. He reserves this sincerity for a sermon on the whole armour of God (Ephesians 6:10) and "If we say we have no sin, we deceive ourselves, and the truth is not in us" (I John 1:8), in which he argues against grandstanding on the side of truth in a time of war. His argument develops from the notion that he knows no one who previously harboured any evil disposition towards those who are now identified as enemies. He attempts to distinguish between the government that has declared war and the people who have not, but acknowledges that the government is not distinct from the populace, without whom no government can act. He notes that the population is taking up arms yet feels no hatred. Nonetheless both the German and Austrian Emperors invoke God in support of their actions. Relying on logic, he, therefore, asks, "Are there two gods, one for us and one for our enemies?" He warns that Christians must be clear that whatever happens will damage what he calls "official" Christianity. Churches exist to prevent "the slaughter of man by man" and, if such slaughter occurs, the Church has failed in its purpose.

Hambly then introduces a personal narrative. Unable to sleep, he had risen early that morning and dressed. He had sat on the wall opposite and gazed across to the church, to "this homely house of God across the roadway" (49), terms which suggest the building serves as a place of comfort and security far removed from the turmoil of nations at war. In dawn's half-light, the church had seemed strange to him. He recounts in his sermon how, in his mind, he compared this church, of which he is so fond, with the great cathedrals of Westminster, Rheims and Paris. Do they, too, look unreal as the sun rises on them? His challenging thought, prompted by this view of his church, is whether we ever see things in their right proportions. Do we see "this curse of war" aright? He makes a sudden move from these thoughts about perception to warn against "taking the prohibitions of the Decalogue in a lump." The sins outlawed therein do not rank equally in God's eye; murdering is ten times worse than breaking the Sabbath.

He displays his personal belief in the pulpit once more when he says that the war is a struggle with principalities and powers, alluding to Ephesians 6 as a specific intertext. Yet the men who go out to fight have seen it from another perspective; often, hunger and no prospect of a better job, rather than any sense of fighting for a noble cause, have led them to enlist. He concludes, "The sins of our enemy are evident. But if *we* say we have no sin, we shall deceive ourselves and the truth will not be in us" (50). The change of tense in the last two clauses of the sentence indicates that the error, while a serious threat, can be avoided. Quiller-Couch's italicised "we" in the quotation above indicates both emphasis and intonation, which highlights one of the problems that occurs when oral texts, such as sermons, migrate into a literary, or chirographic, medium, such as a novel—the loss of the full phonetic quality of words.[21]

By the time Hambly preaches a second sermon, only a week into the war, the novel's readers might think Hambly has gained more confidence as a voice that speaks against the grain, for, after a lengthy quotation of Isaiah 62, Hambly leans forward in the pulpit with his arms resting on the cushion and says, directly, "I want you to apply those words not only to ourselves [. . .] but to the whole of the free peoples of Western Europe" (191). The solemnity and slowness with which he utters these words reinforces their directness. The references Hambly makes in this second sermon range far and wide. In addition to the prophet Isaiah, they include Joshua of the Old Testament, the Roman Emperor who said that the best part of revenge is not to be like those who hurt you, Ecclesiasticus, the philosophical wisdom of Francis Bacon that knowledge is power, an outbreak of typhus in Polpier in the middle ages, and Christ's words about the providence of God. Christ had said that God's providence proves greater than that of human beings, though even they know how to give good gifts to their children. The sermon includes personal points of view, as well as more general expressions of shared faith. Although presented in the novel as a quoted monologue, there are elements of dialogue within it. These include a conversation the preacher has with himself about what a preacher might say, as well as a conversation with his congregation when he anticipates that its members will say that he has,

> ill chosen his time—now, with the enemy at our gates— to be preaching to [them] that [they] should be confirming what little hold [they] have on the divine purpose, to advance upon it; to counsel [their] striving to pierce further into the mind of God; when all the newspapers tell [them] that, for success in war, [they] should enter into the minds of [their] enemies (192).

He posits this potential response to his sermon in order to countermand it. The main proposition of this sermon is that humankind's best chance of knowing God's will is to think as rationally, practically, relevantly and scientifically about ethical and theological matters as scientists think about scientific things (195). On this basis, Hambly has preached a sermon which is cautiously supportive of the war. Without straying away from Christianity to learn a new gospel of hate, he and his hearers, he concludes, should be proud to vindicate what their country has been when at its best (196). On reading this sermon, no one should be surprised that Quiller-Couch called *Nicky-Nan, Reservist* his heat-of-the-moment novel, rushed out in the early months of the Great War. Its specific topicality and themes of international political importance demonstrate the capacity of Methodist sermons in twentieth century novels to be more than evangelical appeals to unredeemed souls.

Moving from troubled preachers, the focus turns to Hamer Shawcross, Howard Spring's fictional political creature in *Fame is the Spur*, who takes his preaching out of the church into the arena of Labour party politics. His crossover from preach to speech compromises genre boundaries and raises the question: what are the essential differences between political oratory and sermons? A comparison of Shawcross's Watchnight sermon and a later soapbox speech demonstrates the compromise.

A telepathic narrator capable of reading the thoughts of both the preacher and his audience (more conventionally, but less accurately, referred to as an omniscient narrator) conveys the Watchnight sermon to the novel's readers. Hamer Shawcross enters boldly and confidently, running up two creaking steps to the platform he will speak from and pausing as if to say without speaking, "Here I am; look at me" (207).

When he smoothes his hair back as he starts to speak, he seems to be smoothing random thoughts into coherent order for his speech. The narrator describes the address as simple, yet imparting to his audience a driving confidence that life still awaited Shawcross and he would grasp it. After the service concludes, Harriet lauds it as a lovely address and he looks back on the year with satisfaction. He senses, nevertheless, that the year ahead would be challenging and alluring.

Shawcross's diary reveals an element of detachment from the people he addresses and will later represent in Parliament, as well as a lack of empathy for their condition. He writes:

> It seemed to me, standing above them, that the year which was about to begin for all these people would hold nothing that the dying year had not held, and that was a bare permission to live, and eat a little, and roughly clothe themselves (208).

Any determination on Shawcross's part to improve their lot does not appear. Shawcross has not linked the religion he espouses with the politics he will soon enter. The "spur" of his political activity begins to be in doubt.

On his political soapbox, his speeches about the representation of the people by the people is later described as "passionate enough preaching" (271), but the rhetoric does not stack up. He tries to associate himself with the poor and unhoused of Ancoats saying, "I have seen you herded in your slums, and what is more I have lived in them with you. I have looked at the houses of the poor with these very eyes of mine in every quarter of the globe." This is powerful, moving rhetoric in which the reader can hear the politician's voice rising. Then the rhetoric collapses with an almost incomprehensible reference to "the clean free sky above me speaking with the immortal encouragement of the stars" (272). In rhetoric both telling and damning, the narrator comments, "No one was quite sure what that last phrase meant, but Hamer Shawcross, riding hell-for-leather on his oratorical mount, didn't give people a chance to think what he meant" (272). These are only words, words, and more words, mere words to fill the space and lure hearers. Many of Hamer's political speeches, known for their use of biblical images and language, illustrate that big words can make nothing much sound important, the tongue-in-cheek criticism made of Hamer's oratory by his opponents.

Of course, such damning judgement should not be made of all who cross the bridge between preaching and political oratory. A clear link exists, and preachers can learn effective techniques for sermons from the study of political speeches. Perhaps the main question about the crossover from preach to speech is where the boundaries lie. Ordinarily a sermon is offered to God as part of a liturgy while ostensibly addressed to a congregation, though it may also feature in an evangelical rally where the liturgy is either informal or slight. Some might say that, when no longer offered to God, the sermon has been degraded into a speech. Skills honed in the pulpit can be transferred to the political arena, as Shawcross consciously does. This is not necessarily the behaviour of a charlatan, as the careers of many actual preacher-turned-political-orators have proved to be. The criticism in *Fame is the Spur* is of one particular fictional politician with impure motivation, and should not be generally applied.

So far, this chapter has described and analysed Methodist sermons in fiction that show contrasting styles of preaching, troubled and troubling preaching, the foundation of Methodist preaching within the ministry of John Wesley and the relationship between political oratory and preaching. To conclude, attention turns to Joseph Hocking's tale of the origins of the British Methodist Church in its current format, *Not One in Ten,* which contains more sermons than any other novel studied herein.

The preacher in *Not One in Ten* is a young minister, Robert Penhale, an enthusiast for Methodist Union. When a local church member, Thirza Bedruthan, first hears him preach, her judgement of his preaching is kept from the reader until she later writes to Penhale. Then she offers the view that he gave the sermon quite nicely, but asks, "What did it amount to truly and really?" She reminds him of Shakespeare's character Hamlet and remarks rather damningly that Hamlet's "Words, words, words" sums up Penhale's preaching: "Words, words, words—a fairly clever little essay without meaning or power" (111). In contrast, Penhale had expected his sermon to result in men and women "deciding for Christ" (44). His own perception of his sermon persisted as an appeal to his hearers to accept the need to follow Christ; Thirza's view is less high-minded.

The novel's third person narrator carefully sets the scene and establishes expectations for the sermon. Thirza, had rarely been in church in the previous year and had never attended a Methodist gathering, most of which had been described to her as lacking decorum and reverence (40). She was surprised, therefore, by the quiet reverence and orderliness of the occasion she attended, though the choir was more enthusiastic than correct and the preacher, who wore no gown, was gentlemanly while lacking dignity (41). Thirza found pleasure in the organ music and enjoyed the hymns. Penhale's prayers were extemporary and, through them, she noticed his sincerity and humility. All this supplies the context for "what struck her most"—the intensity with which the congregation listened to Penhale's sermon, an intensity which was in marked contrast with the "lassitude and seeming indifference" that the sparse parish church congregation usually showed to the vicar's sermons. Thirza judges that Penhale had worked hard in preparing the sermon and had put his best thought into it. At the end of the service, he announced that there would be a prayer meeting, but he was disappointed that more did not stay, as he saw this as a measure of the effectiveness of his preaching. Even so, the local grocer congratulated him on a "grand service" (42). Anyone familiar with Methodist worship in the middle years of the twentieth century will recognise the authenticity of Thirza's account of this service.

The next time one of Penhale's sermons is reported in *Not One in Ten*, he feels tongue-tied as it had been preceded by a carefully-prepared and well-received sermon by a supernumerary minister, Greenwood, who had excelled himself that night. The author gives Greenwood's sermon in free indirect discourse, a representation of what he said without necessarily using the words he would have actually uttered:

> He was anxious, he said, not to tread upon forbidden ground, or to deal with those parts of the subject which belonged to his younger brother Penhale. He, therefore, would deal only with the palpable and the obvious. In order to do this, he went on to show that the various Methodist bodies were, in reality, one. (132)

Free indirect discourse switches naturally to and from the speaker's words and reported speech, and in the case of the narrator's report of this sermon ends with narration; "... he told more than one good story, and, I have said, won great applause from the audience" (133).

Sadly, this undermines Penhale's confidence to such an extent that readers have low expectations of his second sermon. The textual indicators of the preacher's self-awareness are not promising; although he "knows" that the audience was well-disposed to accept the best he could give them, that there was an unsatisfied longing in their hearts, and that they could not have been satisfied with Greenwood's platitudes, he also knew that the speech he had longed to deliver had not come to him. Moreover, he was distracted by Thirza's presence, by his memory of her verdict on his last sermon, and by her companion, the Honourable Alfred Luscombe, her suitor who was displaying total lack of interest in the occasion. He was bored beyond expression. Penhale noted and felt all this as Greenwood spoke, so that when he was introduced as the next speaker, he was only vaguely aware it was his turn to speak. As Penhale stood to speak two facts were clear to him; first, what he wanted to say still eluded him and, second, Thirza was looking at him with an expression of contempt on her face (139). The author chooses to place the speech "offstage," in the gap between the end of chapter thirteen and the beginning of chapter fourteen. As far as the reader is concerned, the speech is thus left unspoken, left to the reader's imagination, and communicated only through the manner in which Hocking sets it up in the novel and Penhale's reported hazy memory of what he said. For instance, he cannot recall that he anonymously referred to Thirza's letter in which her contrary opinion of Methodist Union was expressed, nor that he used John Wesley's words, "The best of all is, God is with us" (141). Like Greenwood, Penhale had excelled himself. If it were not for the author's representation of Penhale's internal thoughts and feelings, as well as his negative awareness of the audience, readers might regard reported reactions to the sermon as indications that Penhale spoke charismatically as a man possessed. The ambivalence of Hocking's depiction of this sermon prevents readers thinking that Penhale was superhuman in his preaching.

When Penhale sets off to preach on Christmas morning, having selected a few old carols people would enjoy singing, he has low expectations. Few people will be in attendance, but the meeting will be pleasant. In fact, he is surprised when he sees that the downstairs portion of the chapel was nearly full and, again, when he hears resonant singing that demonstrates the "gladsomeness of the season" (152). Zacky, the recalcitrant local Penhale has challenged himself to convert, attends the service. Indeed, the concept of challenge is the key that opens understanding of this episode. Quietly, in his thinking, Penhale questions the historicity of Luke's birth narrative, asking whether the shepherds did indeed hear angel songs and whether the truth was anything like the record that had been handed down through the ages. He suppresses these doubts about historicity and drives them from his mind to preach, believing that, if the details could not be trusted, nevertheless "the great Father God had revealed His nature through Jesus Christ" (152). Hocking, in introducing here some of the legacy of biblical criticism, does not sway from either his evangelical zeal or his didactic purposes as an author, as the sermon's conclusion will show. At the end of the sermon, Penhale challenges the church of which he is part to show the truth of all it stands for by saving people from their sins. This way of salvation is quoted in full and followed by the simple observation that Zacky, to whom this specific point is directed, was asleep (154). Previously, Zacky had interrupted the sermon to tell the preacher that, while children might be taken in by some of what he said, grown-up people like him would not be convinced. Penhale ignored the interruptions. The oldest member of the chapel, Jonathan Fletcher, later expresses the view that, as Penhale preached this carefully prepared sermon, he had felt like shouting out as he moved from point to point (179).

On the last Sunday of January 1932, Penhale's preaching impressed Thirza's guest, Miss Trewithen, so much that she proclaimed that she had never heard anyone preach like that before, but Thirza had found it difficult to concentrate on what he said, despite her best efforts. Her mind was distracted by memories of previous conversations, and her eyes were drawn by the handsome fur coat worn by a member of the congregation. Nevertheless, a section of the sermon impressed her. In this section, Penhale anticipates that Methodist Union will be achieved before the end of the year and explains that he has written to all ministers he can think of to ask them, first, how often they have referred to Union when preaching during 1931 and, second, have they made the matter a subject for prayer in their churches. He expresses disgust that of those who have bothered to reply, most have said they do not attribute sufficient importance to the matter either to speak of it or to pray about it. After standing for almost a minute in silence, Penhale says, "That is a terrible, *terrible*, TERRIBLE confession" (189). The shift to italics then to upper case letters indicates rising inflexion in his voice.

At a weeknight service, which had been advertised as not being a preaching service, there was a revival that "was said to be altogether different from any revival services known for generations. There were no appeals to fear; neither was any excitement manifest" (273), but Penhale feels compelled to speak. He believes that the Spirit of God has been speaking to the local population through the evangelical campaign revival and declares that now is the time they should acknowledge it. He specifically names Zacky Krust; "God calls upon you, Zacky, to do according to his will" (273). Then Penhale falls to his knees, a minute passes in silence and Zacky stands to declare his decision "to do the straight thing now" (274).

Soon after Penhale has fulfilled his self-given challenge in this way, he also realises that "human love is not for him" (288). The peace of mind accompanying his realisation that his love for Thirza will never be requited finds expression in the sermon he preaches that night. "Thirza had placed a cold hand upon his heart by escaping from him" but his sermon "became laden with the love of God" (289), and he felt that "he had never known such Power as he felt that night" (290). Hocking, in what twenty-first century readers would regard as blinkered, even inhuman, single-minded devotion to church work, sees this fulfilment in ministry as compensation for the loss of a woman's love.

The sermon given the most coverage in the novel is one Penhale preaches on the first Sunday of Christmas, when a congregation much smaller than had gathered on Christmas Day did not dishearten the minister who, nonetheless, preached with vigour. In "Was It Real to Him?" Hocking sets out the main thrust of the sermon in three sections of direct quotations interspersed with narrative in which the author communicates something of the audience's response and the preacher's thoughts. The narrator directly quotes four paragraphs of the sermon, in which Penhale, first, recapitulated what he had said on Christmas morning; second, repeated his view that Methodist Union was the greatest event in the Christian Church since the Reformation; and, third, spoke of the contribution Methodism had made to Cornwall (164). Penhale's slow, deliberate delivery of the sermon increases the attentiveness of the audience. Hocking switches to indirect speech to narrate the next section of the sermon in which Penhale outlines the impact the arrival of Methodism had on Cornwall—a great ethical and spiritual revolution. Penhale also told of outbreaks of petty strife and quarrelling that fractured Cornish Methodism before describing the dream of reunion that some had begun to foster in the early years of the twentieth century. The next quoted section concerns this dream and Penhale's own commitment to it. Hocking's narrative breaks into the sermon to describe a visible change that came over the preacher; a new light shone in his eyes and his voice became charged with meaning (166). In a third, short quoted passage Penhale, tells of the Methodist Church's failure to catch the vision before he stands in silence looking into distant emptiness. Whether or not this is intended histrionic oratory in the manner of a "divine dramatist" as the early Methodist evangelist, George Whitefield, has been called,[22] its effect makes the audience more watchful and awaits his next words. The words they have waited for are quoted in a final section of the sermon beginning with the question, "What is the use of Methodism? Why does it exist?" These are the very questions actually posed in Kenneth Howcroft's Presidential address at the 2014 Methodist Conference. In the novel, Penhale answers that it exists for the conversion of people, and, if conversions do not result from Union, then Union has failed (166). Penhale then tells Zacky Krust's story before stating John Wesley's claim that Christ saves people to the uttermost; "[h]e stated again and again that it was the centre and circumference of his faith" (167). Thus, because Wesley and his preachers possessed power, Penhale claims, according to the Halevy thesis, England was saved from revolution. They possessed power because they prayed. Again Penhale stood silently. Although many in the audience thought he still had more to say, he announced the last hymn, invited everyone to a New Year's Night prayer meeting, and pronounced the Benediction.

What does the preaching amount to in *Not One in Ten* ? It provides an expression of Joseph Hocking's own understanding of the purpose of preaching and the calling of the Methodist Church. Penhale's ministry is modelled on what Hocking believed the minister's role should be. Hocking exercised his ministry mainly in deprived areas of England. As a minister of the United Methodist Free Church, he served first in Birstall in Leicestershire before moving south to serve for two years in Chelsea and a further seven in Thornton Heath. In both of these London stations, poverty was rife in the closing years of the nineteenth century. From there, he and his family moved to Burnley in Lancashire for three years before returning south in 1898 to take up appointment in a single church circuit in Woodford Green in Essex. This was his first appointment in what he called a "well-to-do suburb." He remained there until the Conference reluctantly accepted his resignation on the grounds of impaired health in 1909. According to Alan Kent, from whose book on the Hocking siblings the course of Joseph's ministerial itinerary has been garnered, ill health was not the sole reason for his resignation.[23] Woodford Green Church's torpor frustrated him, and he did not feel as challenged by the work as he had been in his previous stations. For Joseph Hocking, as for the fictional Penhale, the minister's role was to bring people to Christ where lives will be changed and human society improved.

The last verses of most of Wesley's hymns end in heaven. Similarly, the end of Methodist preaching, as Hocking presents it, is heaven, and his preachers long for trumpet voices to call on all the world to come to "the Saviour of all humankind", originally "the general Saviour of mankind," where there is enough for all, enough for each, enough forevermore.[24] Other novelists show more interest in preaching when it falls short of this ideal and more interest in preachers who struggle to attain it. This paints a complex portrait of Methodist preaching for readers, who are unaccustomed to hearing actual Methodist preaching, to appreciate. In some of these novels, the preaching is manipulative and forbidding; in others, it is ineffective and hindered by ineptitude; in yet others, it is marred by the impure motives of the speaker. Sadly, in only a few is Methodist preaching as liberating and life-giving as it is meant to be:

> Help us your mercy to extol,
> Immense, unfathomed, unconfined. [25]

CONCLUSION

TO SERVE THE PRESENT AGE

Despite George Eliot's best efforts, Methodism has become for some novelists a convenient cipher for repressive religious hypocrisy in English fiction since 1890. Very few novels depict Methodism entirely sympathetically. Identifying even one that depicts it in its current form is difficult. Novelists have not been attracted in large numbers to the contemporary Methodist Church as a setting for their novels. The three principal reasons for this are, first, that, because Methodism is less hierarchical than other Christian traditions, it holds less interest in terms of its political structure and is therefore less hospitable to narratives about ambitious rivalries. Second, Methodism is less clearly defined theologically than Catholicism or fundamentalist groups. Jokes were made about the slimness of Rupert Davies's book entitled *What Methodists Believe*, and this implies that the denomination is less open to fictionalised discussion of belief and less hospitable to fictionalised conflict between faith and experience than other denominational groupings. Third, Methodist congregations are often less representative of the local neighbourhood than parish congregations and can be less diverse, so the Methodist Church is not as attractive to novelists as the setting for books where a broad spectrum of characters is required. As a result, novels exploring the tensions of religious belief in secular times—and there are many—are more naturally set in churches of other Christian traditions.

To state the obvious, all the books in this study, including the fictionalised biography *Hetty Wesley*, are made up. In common with all other fiction, they construct worlds, characters, events and stories, and, to no one's surprise, they make a confusing picture. The novels of Bennett, Carr, Hobbs, Hocking, Kaye-Smith, Quiller-Couch, Spring and Unsworth depicted a range of both self-righteous and righteous men and women who were often religiously idealistic, yet who were forced to live in a world that demanded compromises. Some of their characters are admirable for their courage and devotion to duty and learning, whilst others invite derision for their misplaced zeal. Those who are kindly and attractive are often portrayed as ineffectual, whereas others are willing to do almost anything to achieve their own ends. For some of them, laudatory desire for spiritual and social holiness tips over into religious intolerance and hypocrisy. Of course, fiction plays loose with the truth—summarising, changing perspective, foreshortening, lengthening, using fragments to give an illusion of completeness—and writers give readers a range of images in their fiction from which they can construct imagined characters, worlds and events that are often referred to as if they are real. Because fiction shapes the imagination in these ways, an examination of the portrayal of Methodists and Methodism in fiction has implications for the actual Methodist Church in Britain.

Most nineteenth-century novelists who were not Nonconformists gave the impression that any connection between Nonconformity and modern life could not be maintained, whilst Dissenters rapidly became an anachronistic feature of contemporary society.[1] Throughout the twentieth century, this trend has continued apace. As a result, Methodism in recent fiction seems old-fashioned and remains wedded to a lifestyle and theology more appropriate for an earlier age. In fictional expressions, literature troubles Christianity. In particular, it troubles contemporary Methodists whose calling, as described by Charles Wesley in the hymn from which this Conclusion's title is taken, is to serve the present age.

Because the novels treated in this study inform the public's imagination and conjure for readers a picture of the Methodist Church, they form a small part of the tradition that the contemporary expression of Methodism draws on. The greater parts of that tradition are its actual history and its theology as expressed in its official documents, its preaching and the opinions of individual Methodists recorded in organs such as its national newspapers (now reduced to one—*The Methodist Recorder*). Contemporary Methodists build on this tradition as scholars of the present age stand on the shoulders of their giant predecessors. However, some commentators have concluded that, since Methodist Union in 1932, there has been "a marked discomfort about the usefulness of Methodism's traditional doctrines and practices, even within the Church itself."[2] Early twenty-first century Methodists might marvel that, despite all doom merchants and gainsayers, the British Methodist Church is "yet alive", but most also acknowledge that the time has come for British Methodism to realign how it stands in relation to its tradition.

Like all Christian denominations, the British Methodist Church is a theological movement, but its purpose is more than that of articulating a theological system. Nevertheless, its distinctive theology determines the nature of its purpose. The challenges facing any church in Britain today include the many religious faiths represented in the population, the proximity of other cultures, competing convictions, fractured communities, the violence of distorted religious expressions, the offence of fundamentalisms, increasing spiritual curiosity with little or no obvious means of organised expression, and creeping secularisation. Methodism's Arminian theology, by which the belief that God's love and grace are for the entire world without distinction, discrimination or qualification, equips it in a distinctive way for mission in such a world. Its theology gives Methodists the belief that God's prevenient grace is already active in all of human life, and that they do not *take* God anywhere, but rather seek God's presence already going ahead of them. This provides for open, free, and creative engagement with the world.[3] This attitude does not come across strongly in the novels discussed in this text, although such a stance is evident in Wesley's open air preaching in *Hetty Wesley*, in the concept of *The Tramping Methodist* and among the Methodist politicians in *Fame is the Spur*. The social conscience of Methodism has not been entirely overlooked in these books.

As the twentieth century drew to a close, one of Methodism's historians, John Munsey Turner, listed four components of Methodism's continuing role into the current century, which he believed derived from its history: a prophetic witness to society, a reasoned defence of the Christian faith based on the Wesleyan Quadrilateral of tradition, scripture, experience and reason, the use of groups to nurture faith, and a flexible church structure geared to mission.[4] To this, the Arminian emphasis of its theology, a profound conviction that human society can be transformed and a spirituality that finds its best expression in hymnody can be added. These characteristics all find expression among the Methodists imagined in these novels.

If the contemporary British Methodist Church is to respond to the mixed images of Methodism in English fiction since 1890, it must begin by addressing the nature of its existence. Does it continue to be a society with a clearly defined membership, a discipleship movement in the style of Wesley's Oxford Holy Club, or a church joyfully embracing diversity? As novelists have highlighted a dichotomy between Methodism and the world in which its representatives live, so British Methodism, responding to its novelistic depiction at the beginning of the twenty-first century, must realign how it stands in relation to its tradition. Are Methodists to be guardians of a tradition with its roots in the 1700s or Christians whose theology and spirituality fund living faithfully in the present age? In timely sociological research into the decline in churchgoing and its impact on the Methodist Church, Philip Richter and Leslie Francis argued for a Methodist Church that resists the temptations to offer easy answers, to become more conservative in its teaching, and to retreat from its commitment to work for the betterment of society.[5] The future path of Methodism in Britain does not promise to be easy. Its officers and representatives can learn from its depiction in recent novels and adopt a stance that expresses the best traditions of liberal, socially committed Christianity, attractive to the people in contemporary society. Today's populations, although suspicious of religious certainty, are searching for life's significance with a sense that meaning lies in the spiritual dimension. So they look to literature and the other arts, for significance and meaning are all art's concerns.

Stern, austere and zealous fictional Methodists serve good dramatic, narratival and satirical purpose, but their presence on the page must be countered by the presence of a different type of Methodist in the real world. Where the liberal, open-minded Arminian emphases have been lost or neglected among contemporary Methodists, these characteristics cry out to be re-appropriated. The discrepancies and wide gap between the Methodism depicted in English fiction and the actual British Methodist Church provide a source of measured relief, but some literary advocacy remains to be done both to convince readers of the value of religious faith and to persuade the Methodist Church of Britain how best to serve the present age. Then the made-up stories that constitute novels may achieve the status and goal of all fiction, which is that they will become make-believe and convince readers of the truths they hold.

APPENDIX

AN ANALYTICAL KIT FOR THE LITERARY CRITICISM OF SERMONS IN FICTION

The peculiarity of fictional sermons as a literary genre calls for an analytical method which examines the sermon's audiences, the preacher, the sermon's argument or narrative and its language. In other words, an adaptation of the classical rhetorical lenses of *pathos*, *ethos*, *logos* and *praxis*, where, classically, *pathos* is understood to relate to a text's audience's ability to be moved, *ethos* is understood to relate to the character of the speaker, *logos* is understood to relate to the argument or rationale of the speech, and *praxis* is the working in concert of *pathos*, *ethos* and *logos*, the polyphonic coming together of all aspects of rhetorical technique in heteroglot texts, would assist.[1] The required analytical process derives from the discipline of rhetorical narratology, in whose terminology, in the case of fictional sermons, *pathos* is concerned with the audience or narratee, *ethos* with the preacher or narrator, *logos* with the narrative or flow of the sermon and *praxis* with its language.

The analytical kit begins with introductory questions designed to identify a starting place for the analyst, with the expectation that answers to these will determine which aspects of the sermons require prior analysis. The remaining questions can be considered in any order. The assumption behind the first question is that sermons, as texts that set out to persuade hearers to take a particular course of action or adopt a particular belief, have a function whilst the second assumes that the text under scrutiny has form. In answering the first question, it is important that the analyst tries to distinguish between how the fictive preacher understands the aim and purpose of the sermon and how the author understands them, as well as to recognise that what is apparent to the analyst at this initial stage may need to be revised in the light of what is revealed later. The notion that all theology is persuasive argument underpins much of both the actual practice of preaching and the doing of theology in that, wherever theology is written or spoken, we are not dealing with the description of, or assertions about, commonly-agreed truth; rather, we are dealing with argument and attempts to convince. Theologians—both in the classroom and the pulpit—are attempting to persuade audiences. Rhetorical acts such as sermons, lectures and academic treatises can bear several different forms of persuasion:[2] they can seek to produce a virtual experience, to alter perception, to explain something that has happened, to formulate belief, to initiate action and to maintain action. However, for the sake of economy of effort and manageability when applying rhetorical studies to the art of preaching this checklist streamlines possible suasory intentions down to three organising questions of fact, value and policy: when preaching a sermon, is the preacher intending to persuade listeners to accept a certain way of presenting the facts, to accept or reject the value of a particular worldview or to act in such a way as to implement a particular policy? Identifying the rhetorical purpose of the sermon in this way readily leads to a brief account of its structure, using the terms of optional and obligatory shifts in narrative direction. These are concepts familiar to homileticians, such as David Buttrick who, in his theory of preaching, called these shifts in the plot of a sermon "moves."[3]

To achieve a full appreciation of the form and function of sermons in novels, literary analysts might apply the following set of questions to the text.

What are the **aims and purpose** of this sermon, as understood by both the author and the fictive preacher? Is the persuasive intent of the sermon that the listeners accept an explanation, that they value a particular world-view or that they act in such a way as to implement a policy?

Outline the structure of the sermon, indicating optional and obligatory **shifts of narrative direction.**

1. Pathos

1.1 **Addressivity.** What indications in the text are there that the speaker is accounting for addressees? Who are the sermon's:

- intratextual actual audience
- intratextual implied audience
- extratextual actual audience
- extratextual implied audience?

Is there a wider audience this fictional preacher is consciously addressing?

1.2 What **schemata** are being relied on in the text? What background knowledge do the author and reader share? How are schemata preserved, reinforced or refreshed? If refreshed, are there examples of schema destroying, constructing or connecting and with what interpretative consequences?

1.3 Identify any **Face Threatening Acts** in the sermon. How are they mitigated? What positive and negative **politeness phenomena** are used?

2. *Ethos*

2.1 Note intratextual and contextual **performance frames** especially paralinguistic features such as pitch, pause and stress, formulae such as conventional openings and endings, appeals to tradition and the use and range of figurative language, as well as contextual features such as dress, place and time. Are there any performance frames which suggest that the preacher thinks (s)he is presenting the Word?

2.2 **Point of view**. Who conveys the sermon to the reader: is it a fictional hearer, a fictional preacher or the novelist? What value-laden expressions are used? Are there any indicators of the internal representation of the fictional preacher's thoughts or perceptions, such as verbs of perception and cognition, verbs related to factivity, modal verbs and adverbs related to factivity?

2.3 **Proxemics**. How is space used in this gathering? Is it formal, therefore sociofugal or is it flexible, therefore sociopetal?

2.4 **Preacher status.** What is the preacher's adopted role and tone—subordinate, peer or superior to addressees? Does the preacher construct a virtuous persona within the speech? How does the rhetor demonstrate competence, trustworthiness and dynamism? Is there any evidence, both within the sermon and elsewhere in the novel, to suggest that the sermon's capacity to persuade is compromised by the preacher's reputation? What contextual and textual indicators of the preacher's self-awareness are there? Is the preacher inspired, inspiring, doubting, speaking against or expressing the 'party line'?

3. *Logos*

3.1 What sort of **reasoning** is used in this oratory—practical (*phronesis*) or universal (*episteme*)? What supporting materials, that is to say data and warrants, are used in this sermon to support its aim? Note especially references to the Church Fathers, classical Christian doctrine, the prayerbook and theological authorities. In particular how is the Bible used?

3.2 **Intertextuality** and textual density. What are the texts behind, before, around and after this sermon? Identify explicit, implicit and inferable intertexts.

3.3 What **response-inviting techniques** are employed in these fictive sermons?

3.4 **Worldview**. What possible world does this discourse create? What elements of the dominant theology, residual elements from the old order and elements of an emergent new order are you able to identify within the sermon?

4. *Praxis*

4.1 **Speech forms**. Is the sermon narrated or quoted? Note how the author uses direct, indirect and free indirect discourse. If there is an anterior speech position (that is, an actual sermon behind the fictional one), consider how the author has changed the sermon when translating it into the fictional world of the novel, noting especially the occurrence of rhetorical figures in the text, their retention from the actual sermon by the novelist and their adjustment or elision from the written text.

4.2 **Lexis**. Is the vocabulary simple or complex, evaluative or descriptive, general or specific? What are the associations of any idioms in the text? Note any rare, archaic or specialised words? Apply the same test to syntax, using sentences, clauses and phrases as the structure of inquiry.

4.3 **Intonation**. How does the novelist communicate the expressive aspect of the sermon's language? Are there any tone-setting authoritative utterances?

4.4 **Pragmatics**. What direct and indirect speech acts are in the sermon? Note constatives (which may be implicitly performative) and performatives in the text. Is the intended effect achieved?

Some brief notes on the above analytical kit prove necessary. The first section is to do primarily with the facility of modern readers to engage with the literary and rhetorical art of preaching that increasingly fewer of them actually encounter in the real world. Critical to this audience appreciation and the fictional preacher's success in addressing such a non-churchgoing readership is the novelist's facility with schemata. These relate to the way readers use memory to carry information from one story to another, to assist in making meaning of new and unfamiliar situations in stories.[4] Schemata provide information and background knowledge shared by readers and writers, which enable successful negotiation around the scenes and scripts of texts.[5] For instance, although I have no experience of life in eighteenth-century England, I can use schemata, that is organised representations of background knowledge gleaned from history lessons, other historical novels and television programmes, to interpret Quiller-Couch's fictionalised account of the Wesley family in *Hetty Wesley.* Similarly someone who has never been to a contemporary church service may nevertheless engage with a novel's account of a Christian act of worship. The schemata brought to a particular text are usually prompted by intratextual triggers, but the scale to which readers employ schemata is determined by, and dependent upon, the reader.[6] In some texts, schemata are merely reinforced unchanged as interpretative aids for readers; in others, they are preserved by the addition of further information; in yet others, schemata are refreshed. This usually requires disruption of expectations, which cannot be total, as too drastic or too sudden changes tend to lead readers to reject the discourse as unreliable or incredible. Examples of this might be the clergyman who rejects every aspect of religion, though many fictional clergymen can reject almost all. Refreshed schemata effect change and disrupted schemata can result in the destruction of existing, often moribund or clichéd, schemata, the construction of new ones or the establishment of new connections between existing schemata. Consideration of the schemata of preaching in novels reveals how assumed "norms" in preaching, or mental typifications within the setting of churches,[7] are established, parodied or challenged in novels.

The second section of the analytical kit gives cause to consider the status of the preacher. Augustine of Hippo regarded this aspect of oratory a major rhetorical factor because he believed the quality of a speaker's life had greater persuasive weight than his or her eloquence.[8] For him *ethos* was much more than whatever virtue was established by the speaker within the speech itself. Whether intentionally or not, Augustine was adopting the view of the Isocratic school of rhetoric which argued that virtue could only be reflected in speeches when the speaker was truly virtuous.[9] This is in apparent contradiction with New Criticism's critical approach to texts. New Critics dismiss what they call "the intentional fallacy" with Michel Foucault's question "What matter who's speaking?"[10] whereas the prevailing culture of suspicion towards authority is strongly pro-Augustinian in that most people expect priests and politicians to practise what they preach. The way those who profess belief in God conduct their lives, and how those lives are perceived by their audiences, have significant effect on how their preaching is received. Think of the cases of Paul Tillich, whose reputation was damaged by revelations of sexual impropriety in his wife's autobiography, and, in contrast, of Dietrich Bonhoeffer, whose martyrdom put into practice all he had been proclaiming in his preaching and his writing, and it is plain to see that it is not only character itself, but the audience's judgement of the speaker's character that persuades. However, the evidence to support this assertion is not absolute, for different people judge differently. A further complicating factor comes with the influence on the response when readers recognise that a speaker is pretending or dissembling. [11]

However, preaching has a necessarily performative aspect, to which British homileticians, such as Alec Gilmore,[12] as well as American homileticians, such as Jana Childers,[13] have drawn attention. In both the theatre and church, distance creates an arena for something to happen.[14] In Bakhtinian terms the preaching act may be centrifugal, comparable to a play performed under a proscenium arch, or centripetal, comparable to the more flexible theatrical experience of a play in an intimate theatre in the round. Drama theory prefers the terms sociofugal and sociopetal.[15] At various points in this book, the problematic of theatricality, performance, histrionics and pretence has been crucial when assessing the novelist's representation of preacher's integrity, or lack of it.

The third section turns to the argument of the sermon. Aristotle distinguished between *episteme*, which is formal logic, undisputed, universal and eternally applicable in all situations, and *phronesis* which is related to practical reasoning and which attempts to apply logic, which may be variable, to specific circumstances. In Aristotelian rhetoric, this distinction between *episteme* and *phronesis* is central to an understanding of the nature of rhetorical argument. Aristotle showed that rhetorical argument is like logical argument, except in that, whereas logical argument offers a major and minor premise which, if both are accepted, lead to a logically valid conclusion, rhetorical argument leaves out one of the premises (usually the major premise). Speaker and listener alike then must assume this unstated premise if the argument is to be accepted. In the late 1950s Stephen Toulmin expanded and amplified Aristotle's approach and described our everyday use of argument in what he called "working logic."[16] Many of the arguments made in the pulpit, in academia, and in courts of law use this working logic or practical reasoning rather than the formalities of *episteme*. Toulmin showed how, when we argue, we present a claim, which is supported by data and backed by warrants, where the movement from data to claim in an argument is dependent upon, or underpinned by, warrants. These are the underlying, usually implicit but crucial supports, on which the success or failure of a rhetorical argument stands or falls. According to Toulmin, warrants are crucial because they are often the points in an argument at which hearers disagree with speakers. So analysis of the *logos* of a fictional sermon begins by identifying the data and warrants the speaker marshals in the sermon's rhetorical argument, then notes the preacher's use of authoritative texts. In actual preaching, especially in postmodern society where suspicion of the authority of both scripture and preaching prevails, the preacher's use of authoritative texts—prayerbooks, bibles, the treatises of major theologians and the classical creeds as part of preaching's intertexts—and their relative weighting need to be carefully considered.

A preacher's intended outcome will usually betray his or her worldview.[17] Three forms of worldview may be present in sermons—dominant, residual and emergent worldviews. Sermons may create new meanings, new values and new practices that constitute an emergent world view; they may retain elements of an old order expressed in the conventional theological discourses of hegemonic Christendom (indeed, organised religion has been criticised for being too attached to parent institutions and predominantly residual); and they, through hegemonic preaching, may seek to bolster the dominant world order or the archaic dominant Christian worldview, which has, of course, been described in many ways including the two most common, those being a U-shaped curve of "paradise to loss to restoration" and a line of tension stretched between human freedom and restriction.[18] After all, it can be said that a preacher's task is to create an alternative world for the hearer to inhabit, to fund the Christian imagination to picture a world of kingdom values[19] and to let "Kingdom-come." In other words, sermons, like other rhetorical acts, attempt to move auditors from one place to another, or move them from subscribing to one thought form to another. Sermons attempt to change their hearers' minds. Identifying the worldviews within the text of a sermon will assist in assessing the viewpoint changes that the preacher, whether fictional or actual, intends for the audience.

Lastly, the fourth section brings together all of the above under the heading of *praxis*. This highlights one of the distinctions between sermons and fiction. In novels, most speech is made up; it is without an anterior speech position.[20] However, one of the exceptions to this general rule is the fictional sermon, in at least two ways. In historical novels, actual sermons by historical characters are often used for cultural placing and, in any novel, authors often use sermons they have heard in churches as "models" for the sermons they write. Comparison with a sermon's anterior speech position, if there is one, can be made. Moreover, setting the sermon against the backdrop of other speech forms used by the character elsewhere in the novel can also be done. Classically this can be witnessed in Dickens's Chadband in *Bleak House*, a lay preacher who preaches both in and out of season.[21] Whatever the circumstances, to whomsoever he is speaking and wherever he is speaking, Chadband uses only one speech form often with humorous effect, but, in many other fictional instances, the analyst will observe how characters adapt their forms of speech when preaching. This draws attention to the range of linguistic repertoires available to preachers and others who talk or write about God. The theologian, Karl Barth, distinguished between ecclesiastical language, colloquially referred to as the "language of Canaan", and everyday language or "the speech of Mr Everyman" and argued that, whilst the Church will necessarily have its specific language, preachers must also learn to translate from the distinctive specialised language of the Church, which is essential to the preservation of the church's distinctive identity, into the language of the newspaper.[22] Failure to do this, Barth argued, keeps the church in a snail's shell, unable to engage with the social, economic and political realities of the contemporary world. This was a stark warning, as, at the time Barth wrote, the German Church was emerging from its failure to engage with Nazism. Rarely is this matter of terminology or vocabulary as critical in novels as it was in Barth's own time, yet paying attention to the language of the fictional sermon and what the preacher sets out to achieve, or perform, through the text often uncovers how the novelist intends readers to receive the preacher: is the novelist depicting this preacher as an archaic anachronism or someone capable of relating Christian faith to contemporary life?[23]

This analytical kit can be presented in diagrammatic form, making it more naturally understandable for those more attuned to visual learning. Representing the checklist in diagrammatic form, moreover, retains a sense of the dynamism of the rhetorical act of preaching, avoids the artificiality of sequencing analysis and the implication of priority within the analytical procedure and, provided the chosen entry point was suggested by the answers to the introductory questions and not by the whim of the analyst, removes any implications that the analyst may have distorted the sermon in her or his critique of it. In diagrammatic form, the toolkit is appropriately reminiscent of Gadamer's image of the hermeneutic circle, in which a text's interpreter circles around the text, never able to interpret its end without understanding its beginning and never able to interpret its beginning without understanding its end, although always capable of achieving the interpretative stop of a fusion of the author's and readers' horizons. The diagram thus shows a centrally-situated sermon orbited by four blocks of analytical questions. So the toolkit, in the form used in the analysis of the preaching in the novels central to this study, can be represented by the following diagram:

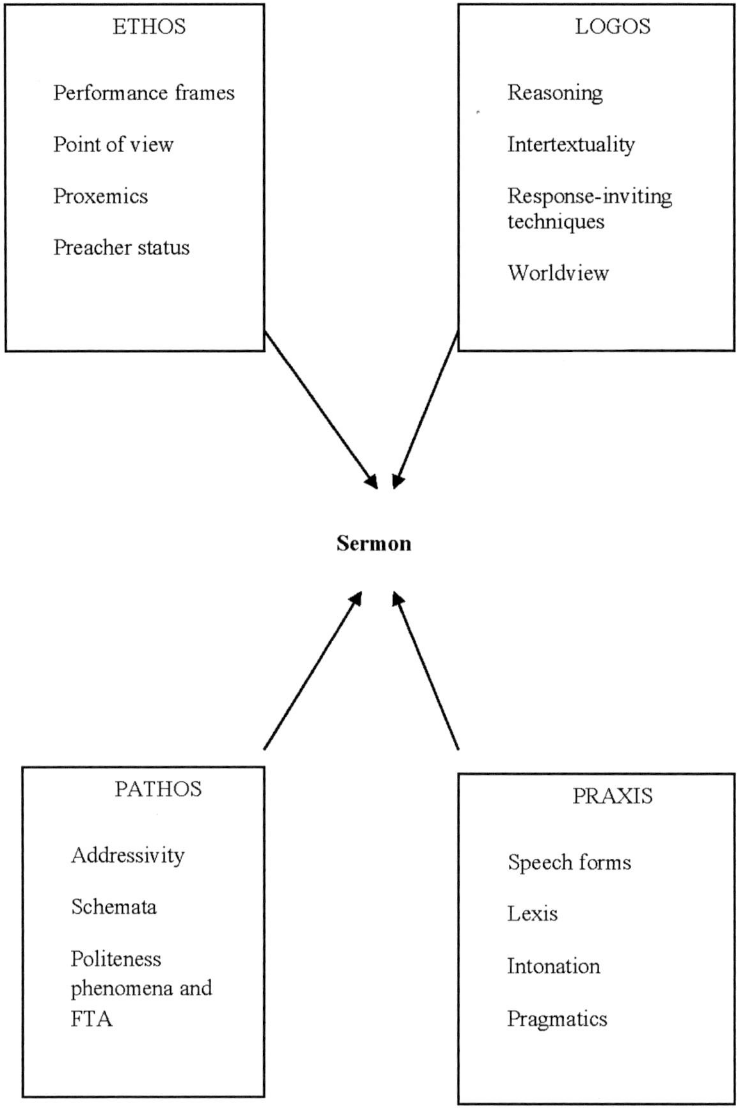
ETHOS
Performance frames
Point of view
Proxemics
Preacher status
LOGOS
Reasoning
Intertextuality
Response-inviting techniques
Worldview
Sermon
PATHOS
Addressivity
Schemata
Politeness phenomena and FTA
PRAXIS
Speech forms
Lexis
Intonation
Pragmatics

NOTES

Introduction

[1] Shepherd, T. B., *Methodism and the Literature of the Eighteenth Century* (London: Epworth, 1940)
[2] Dickinson, D., 2013.
[3] Kent, Alan *Pulp Methodism*, 57.
[4] This was Kent's rather damning judgement in *ibid.,* 213.
[5] McConnell, *The Character of Methodism, passim.*
[6] Parrinder, *Nation and Novel*, 288.
[7] Bennett, *Anna of the Five Towns,* 31.
[8] Crabbe, *The Borough,* xiv.
[9] Davies, S. *Awakening.* Quotation noted from e-book read 12/04/ 2015.
[10] Named after Jacobus Arminius, a Dutch Reformed theologian, who lived from 1560 to 1609.
[11] This was the only prerequisite for admission to the Methodist class meetings in the time of the Wesleys.
[12] *Singing the Faith,* 401.
[13] *Ibid.,* 358.
[14] *Ibid.*, 320.
[15] *Ibid.*, 436.
[16] Green, S. J. D., *The Passing of Protestant England: Secularisation and Social Change c. 1920 – 1960* (Cambridge: Cambridge University Press, 2011)
[17] Source: R. Currie et al., Churches and Churchgoers: Patterns of Church Growth in the British Isles since 1700 (1977), Table A3, 139-144, and Notes, 145-146.
[18] Martin, D., *Religion and Power*, 11.
[19] See Bruce, S., *Secularization* for a full discussion of these points.
[20] Martin, *op. cit.,* 240.
[21] Kitcher, P., *Life after Faith.* 124.
[22] The journals were accessed on 8 January 2016 –
http://www.publications.parliament.uk/pa/ld200506/ldjournal/239/060.htm#1
http://www.publications.parliament.uk/pa/cm200506/cmjournal/262/commons_journal_262.pdf
[23] Williams, R., *Faith in the Public Square.* 15
[24] *Ibid.,* 2.
[25] *Ibid.,* 7.
[26] Wood, J., *The Nearest Thing to Life*
[27] See Anderson, M. G., *Imagining Methodism in 18th-century Britain.,* 236 and 238 for a concluding comment on this phenomenon in relation to Anderson's discussion of Methodism in 18th century fiction and her justification for reading 18th century literature as a basis for understanding our current age.

[28] Cupitt, D., *What is a Story?* 41
[29] See my discussion of biblical fiction in 'Lest the story be lost: biblical fiction' in Prickett, S., ed. *The Edinburgh Companion to the Bible and the Arts,* 109-110
[30] Matz, J., *The Modern Novel.,* 134 and 136
[31] James, H., *Henry James: Literary Criticism.* 129-33
[32] Matz, op cit., 32
[33] Ibid., 33
[34] Ibid., 44
[35] Op. cit., 67
[36] See Matz,, 40 for a brief discussion of this.
[37] See my *The Novel as Church* for a discussion of this almost anachronistic phenomenon.

1. Our high calling's glorious hope

[1] Cunningham, V., 60
[2] *Not One in Ten,* 83
[3] See Herbst, M. T. "The Pernicious Effects of Novel Reading"
[4] See Winchester C. T., (1905) 372-374
[5] Shepherd, 216
[6] Anderson, M. G., 32
[7] Shepherd, 224
[8] Hamlet, Act V sc. i
[9] Sterne, L. *The Sermons of Mr Yorick,* vii
[10] Cash, A. H. "The Sermon in Tristram Shandy" 400
[11] Ibid., 408
[12] Ibid., 417
[13] Cunningham, V., 115
[14] Harrison, G. E., *Haworth Parsonage*
[15] Cunnningham, 124
[16] Harrison, G. E. *The Clue to the Brontës* 167ff.
[17] Nash, J. and B. S. Suess, *New Approaches to the Literary Art of Anne Brontë.*
[18] Ogawa, K.,"Religious Sensibility in Anne Brontë's *Agnes Grey* and *The Tenant of Wildfell Hall*"
[19] Parrinder, G., *The Great Novelist of English Religion.*79.
[20] Quoted by Parrinder,.81.
[21] McConnell II, J. E. "The Character of Methodism in George Eliot's *Adam Bede*"
[22] Cunningham, 152
[23] Ibid., 248
[24] *Minutes of Several Conversations at the Sixtieth Annual Conference* (Manchester, England, July 25th 1803), 33-34, quoted in McConnell, 252
[25] Quoted in Ashton, R., "Lunch with the Rector"
[26] Church, L., *The Early Methodist People*
[27] McConnell, 253

2. The Millennial year rushes on to our view

[1] Parrinder, *Nation and Novel*, 288
[2] Bennett, *Anna of the Five Towns,* 31
[3] Price Hughes, D., "The Novels of Mr Arnold Bennett and Wesleyan Methodism"
[4] Miller, L. P., "Casting Graven Images: *The Damnation of Theron Ware."*
[5] Myers, R. M., "Antimodern Protest in *The Damnation of Theron Ware."*
[6] Zimmerman, D. H., "Clay Feet, Modernism and Fundamental Option in Harold Frederic's *The Damnation of Theron Ware."*
[7] Roberts, S. C., ed. *Memories and Opinions of Q: An unfinished autobiography*

3. On mercy's wings I swiftly fly

[1] Quoted in Wakefield, G. S., *Methodist Spirituality*, 26
[2] Scotland, Nigel A. D., 'Methodism and the English Labour Movement 1800-1906' in *Anvil,* Vol. 14 No 1, 1997, pp. 36-48.
[3] Quoted in Scotland, *op. cit.,* p. 46.
[4] Quiller-Couch, Arthur, *Memories and Opinions,* 40
[5] Quoted in Spring, M. H., *Howard,* 177
[6] *Ibid.,* 38
[7] *Ibid.,* 39
[8] *Ibid.,* 40
[9] *Ibid.,* 41
[10] *Ibid.,* 41-2
[11] *Ibid.,* 43
[12] Hardy, T., *Satires of Circumstance*, 51

4. Enough for evermore

[1] In a private email exchange in January 2014
[2] In the same email exchange as above
[3] Gordon, E., "The author of *The Short Day Dying* who unexpectedly became a writer during a long illness" http://www.newstatesman.com/books/2008/03/hobbs-sentimentality downloaded 15/08/2012
[4] Brett, M., "*In the English Lower Depths: Sid Chaplin's Newcastle novels"*
[5] In an interview with the author, 11th November 2014
[6] In *A Credo*, he wrote "(life) is about something, it isn't meaningless." (178)
[7] Op. cit., 21
[8] In "City of God how broad and far outspread thy walls sublime!"' *Hymns and Psalms* 809

5. O for a trumpet voice on all the world to call

[1] Arditti, M., *Easter*, 375-377. See also my discussion of the Methodist antecedents to this sermon and the influence of Methodism on the young Arditti in *The Novel as Church,* 39
[2] Swales, J. M., *Genre Analysis,* 25-27
[3] This term is taken from Guy Cook's description of the cornerstone of Russian formalism *ostranenie* in his *Discourse and Literature*, 131
[4] Bakhtin, M. M., "Speech Genres", 60
[5] Bakhtin, M. M., *The Dialogical Imagination*, 261
[6] These roughly equate with the classical rhetorical tools of pathos, ethos, logos and praxis which come together to form an analytical toolkit described in the Appendix.
[7] The analytical checklist discussed in the appendix is in tabular form, but frequent use has shown that different starting points in the checklist for different sermons are more appropriate. There can be no common entry point. In this case, our analysis begins with the sermon's argument.
[8] Quoted in Cunningham, V., 157
[9] Homileticians on both sides of the Atlantic have exploited the comparison to improve preachers' techniques. See, for instance, Alec Gilmore's *Preaching as Theatre* and, from the United States, Jana Childers's, *Performing the Word: Preaching as Theatre*
[10] See Anderson M. G. for a discussion of Foote's satires *The Minor* in her *Imagining Methodism in Eighteenth-Century Britain*, 130
[11] The semiotics of theatre and drama more conventionally use the terms sociofugal and sociopetal. See Elam, K., *The Semiotics of Theatre and Drama*, 64
[12] All preachers, in some way, take account of their audience. Theologians, in their writing, lecturing and preaching, tend to construct their discourses on the basis of one of four ways of understanding their audience: they either intentionally specify the audience they are addressing (perhaps other academic theologians or new students of theology), make an empirical analysis of the audience and address the actual hearers, address an imagined pluralist composite audience or address an idealised universal audience they have imagined. (See Cunningham, D., *Faithful Persuasion,* 204ff.). Conventional rhetorical narratology speaks of three different audiences–first, a book's authorial audience who are the hypothetical potentially-corrupted readers with beliefs, values, reading practices and prejudices, second, a book's narratival or narrating audience who are the imaginary, idealised audience for whom the author is writing and, third, a book's actual audience who are the people who actually read the book. (See Kearns, M., 51-55 for a discussion of this). In the case of oral texts such as political speeches, lecture and sermons, there is a further complication. They also have primary and secondary addressees. Sermons are both "church talk" and "public talk" in that the preacher addresses both the congregation present in the church and a wider public beyond. Similarly politicians' speeches at political rallies address the audience in the room and speak out beyond to the general public who overhear through the media of journalistic reports. In the case of sermons within fiction, at least three levels of audience can

be conceived: the author addressing the reader extratextually, the external narrator addressing the narratee within the text and the fictional preacher in the novel's internal fictional world addressing the fictional congregation. Those who comment on sermons in fiction should look for signs within the fictive sermon that the preacher is taking account of these audiences and identify the constituents of four audiences–the actual audience within the text, the fictional preacher's implied audience, the author's extratextual actual audience and the author's implied audience. The relationship between these audiences can be represented on a scale, where the actual writer addresses the actual reader, the external narrator addresses the narratee and the fictional character addresses his or her audience. None of these is discreet, as each is capable of overhearing the other.

[13] Reputedly these were Aeschines and Demosthenes.

[14] Crudely speaking, success in rhetoric requires the capacity to woo an audience and the speaker often uses politeness phenomena. People everywhere expect politeness, so speakers mitigate the potential impoliteness of Face Threatening Acts (FTA) by using techniques such as indirectness and politeness markers and by taking account of the other person's negative or positive face. For a full discussion of this, see Brown and Levinson, "Universals in Language Usage: politeness phenomena". In some instances there may be a mismatch between the strength of the FTA and the mitigating features employed by the speaker and it can be revealing to speculate on the reasons for any mismatch and any deleterious effects it has caused. Usually this is a matter of the over-polite preacher oozing unctuousness and implying insincerity, but the opposite is true of this unusual example, whose extraordinariness results from Bennett's satirical purpose and disapproval of Methodism. The question of over-politeness is discussed further by Simpson in *Language through Literature*, 176.

[15] An interesting study of the way men and women use language to create an authoritative stance in their preaching was conducted by the sociolinguist Frances Lee Smith in her essay "The Pulpit and Woman's Place: Gender and the Framing of the 'Exegetical Self' in Sermon Performances". She identified three forms of talk, ranging from the light authority of "parenthetical embroidery" to the weightier authority of "high talk", between which there lay a mean of "hyper-smooth delivery". She spoke of preachers' textual selves, which she defined as the person who seems to stand behind the textual statements in the discourse, and spoke also of "textual self-footing" which she understood as the core alignment between the speaker and the audience ... (147). She said that preachers typically display one of three textual selves: either that of an exegeter *[sic]* (for which the conventional British term is exegete, but for a literary critical study of sermons the term "hermeneut" may be preferable); that of an exhorter (for which either "rhetor" or the more familiar "orator" may be preferable); or that of an illustrator (for which "commentator" may be preferable). In any or all of these textual selves, preachers may self-identify as mouthpieces, thus establishing themselves as instruments verbalising the divine will. Such preachers, like Palehouse in Kaye-Smith's novel, are likely to claim to be Spirit-led, or inspired. However, radical Christians such as William Blake long ago distinguished between mouthing scripture and allowing the texts to inspire; the first required memory and, perhaps, reason, whereas the

latter used imagination to re-mint biblical imagery in such a way that what was true for previous generations was now refreshed by hermeneuts who spoke in their own way in their own day. Our current concern is to ascertain which of these roles the Methodists, who preach in the novels under consideration, think they are fulfilling. What we are seeking to discover here is what we might call the "spiritual condition" of the fictional preacher: what is the nature of the relationship the preacher believes he has with his sermon? It might be helpful to rephrase this question: Does the fictional sermon express personal views, the tradition of the church or the biblical tradition? Indeed, is the preacher speaking "beyond himself"? Note the intentional gender-specific language of these questions: all but one of the preachers referred to in this book is male, which raises another intriguing issue–that of the role of women in the church and pulpit. Answers to these questions, when used to interrogate sermons in fiction, are likely to fuel a discussion of the problem of religious authority, which is always intriguing in the context of fiction where authority is rarely absolute.

[16] Performance frames to look out for within the text of fictional sermons will include paralinguistic features such as pitch, pause and stress, formulae such as conventional openings, conventional endings and appeals to tradition and the range of figurative language the preacher uses (as discussed by Bauman in *Verbal Art as Performance*, 21) . Fabb in *Linguistics and Literature* indicates there may also be extratextual performance frames such as dress, place and time, significant because the preacher's attire, the design of the venue and the nature of the occasion will indicate some of the preacher's self-consciousness. Those who listen to sermons when reading a novel containing a sermon might similarly ask where the hearer's ear is attuned: are we being invited to listen to the preacher or to the voice of God above and beyond the preacher? Is the preacher pointing to God or drawing our attention to the performance? We might, therefore, think of these performance frames as constituents of shared knowledge within a tacit contractual relationship between the preacher and congregation. If we do this, then we can see that one of the ways in which this "contract" is threatened is when the performer chooses to perform to a different community or when the community changes, as is the case when sermons are placed in the fictional world of novels and perform to readers. Sermons in fiction are dangerous creatures!

[17] See his *44 Sermons* still used as required doctrinal teaching for trainee Methodist preachers.

[18] Readers are constantly aware that narratives are focalised. Because, as Wayne Booth famously said, when we are reading we cannot forget that we are reading (Booth, 53), we know we are being told a story; the narrative is focalised in that it is oriented through the point of view of a character or a narrator. This is true even in the case of omniscient narrators, although we should exercise caution in using the concept of omniscience to describe narrators who would be better described as narratively authoritative rather than all-knowing, as telepathic in understanding another's inner thoughts, as self-reflexive as the shaper of a tale and as almost superhumanly capable of sagacious reflection on events from several perspectives. See Culler's essay on "Omniscience" in *Narrative*, 32, for a discussion of this. Focalising, a term borrowed from the art of photography perhaps to indicate where

and how a narrator is looking, has arguably a better analogue in the photographer's use of filters for focusing, foregrounding and tinting: similarly narratives are filtered through someone's point of view. Fictional sermons will usually be filtered homodiegetically by a character in the text, perhaps directly by the preacher, or heterodiegetically by a narrator who is absent from the narrative. In either case, the presence of any value-laden expressions, as well as any indicators of either the preacher's or the audience's perception of the sermon, will inflect the reader's reception of the text. What we are looking for is the preacher's, the narrator's or the novelist's "angle of telling." What mosaic of cultural assumptions, beliefs and institutional practices has shaped both the language of the sermon and the novel's report of it?

[19] The matter of intertextuality is fascinating. It concerns the texts behind, before, around and after the main text that trigger evoked references for the reader. Cook discusses the range of intertextuality in *Discourse and Literature*, 172. The density of a text's intertextuality is best established by groups of readers, for, whilst explicit intertextuality is usually part of the writer's self-conscious contribution to the text, some implicit and most inferable intertexts originate in the reader's contributions to the text. The strength of this aspect of the intertextual drive is beyond authorial control. For instance, working with a group of preachers on their response to Christmas sermons written up in an unpublished dissertation in the mid 1990s taught the author that one person's intertextual detour, by which an allusion within a sermon took the hearer beyond self to another place with illuminating or cathartic effect, is sometimes another person's dead end. Because a text may remind one reader of another text, but another reader of yet another text, the never-finished web of intertextuality is complex and unbounded; each new reader adds to it. See Pope's *The English Studies Book,* 247 and Worton and Still's *Intertextuality*. The fictional sermon's relationship with the Christian tradition on the one hand and its contemporary culture on the other will be apparent from its intertextuality. Of course, in the case of novels published some years ago, the sermon's contemporary culture may belong to two eras–that of the intratextual audience and intended readership, as well as that of the actual contemporary reader. Nevertheless, the source of the preacher's allusions in the sermon will reveal the extent of the preacher's rootedness in either the Christian tradition or contemporary culture.

[20] This observation draws on the insights of the French theorist, Gérard Genette, who suggested that there are three main states of speech within novels: "narrated" (where the narrator's word and syntax are used), "transposed" (where the narrator's syntax is used whilst some of the character's words are included) and "reported" (where the character's words and syntax are used, whilst the narrator uses inquit signals). These are occasionally referred to as narrated monologue, psycho-narration and quoted monologue, but the convention is to distinguish between direct speech, where the character speaks, indirect speech where the narrator speaks, and free indirect speech which is both speakerly and speakerless, to use the terms Henry Gates used in *The Signifying Monkey*, 209 and 215. This free indirect speech is a literary bi-vocal language that, in its printed form, no one

could have spoken although the reader is able to recognise its aspiration towards orality.

[21] Bakhtin argued that, although there is always an expressive aspect to all utterances, the expressive intonation tends to belong to the utterance rather than specific words within it. He was, nevertheless, reluctant to abandon altogether the notion that words have "emotional colouring" or "stylistic aura", so in *"Speech Genres"* 86, he argued that we select our words for their inherent emotional tone. Some words may have typical expression; moreover, all epochs, social circles, families, faith communities and interpretive communities have what Bakhtin called "tone-setting authoritative utterances," by which he meant typical utterances which set the standard, one might say neutral, tone conventional to that community, and on the basis of which the expressive element of an utterance can be established. For instance, it is conventional in the Christian Church to describe the persuasive purpose of the four Gospels as *ευαγγελίον*–the telling of good news–but if a preacher were to choose to describe it, as it is lexically legitimate to do, as "propaganda", then that deviation from the tone-setting norm or what Soskice in *Metaphor and Religious Language* (69) calls "accustomed speech," gives the unorthodox choice of word an intonation or expressive element which can be heard even in its written form. Thus, sometimes a sermon's orality can be retained even when set in the amber of literariness.

[22] These are the words of historian Harry S. Stout used as the title of his 1991 biography of Whitefield.

[23] Kent, A. M. *Pulp Methodism*, 109

[24] From Charles Wesley's hymn, "Father, whose everlasting love" (*Singing the Faith* 320).

[25] These lines are also from Charles Wesley's hymn, "Father, whose everlasting love" (*Singing the Faith* 320).

Conclusion: To serve the present age

[1] Cunningham, *Everywhere Spoken Against,* 279

[2] Dean, J. in an essay summing up the opinions of several contributors to Craske *et al. Unmasking Methodist Theology*, 221

[3] See Rebekah Miles's essay for a discussion of the surprising possibilities for interfaith dialogue provided by John Wesley's writings and theology

[4] Turner, J. M. *Modern Methodism in England,* 157-164

[5] Richter and Francis, *Gone But Not Forgotten*, 96.

Appendix

[1] Cunningham, D., *Faithful Persuasion*, 204f. See also Hogan and Reid, *Connecting with the Congregation,* 15, for the origins of what is developed here.

[2] Campbell, K. K., *The Rhetorical Act.*

[3] Buttrick, D., *Homiletic.*

[4] Bartlett, F. C., *Remembering*, 199-201
[5] Short, M., *Exploring the Language of Poems, Plays and Prose*, 228
[6] *Ibid.,* 231 and Cook, G., *Discourse and Literature*, 192
[7] Stockwell, P., *Cognitive Poetics.*
[8] See Robertson, D. W., *op. cit.,* Book 4, sections 4-26.
[9] Hogan and Reid, *op. cit.,* 51
[10] Foucault, M., "What is an Author?", 138
[11] Lose, *Confessing Jesus Christ,* 161f.
[12] Gilmore, A., *Preaching as Theatre.*
[13] Childers, J., *op. cit.*
[14] *Ibid.,* 45
[15] Elam, K., *The Semiotics of Theatre and Drama*, 64
[16] Toulmin, S., *The Uses of Argument.*
[17] This discussion derives from Raymond Williams's discussion of hegemony in *Marxism and Literature.*
[18] Ferretter, L., *Towards a Christian Literary Theory*, 170
[19] Brueggemann, *W.*, *The Bible and the Postmodern Imagination.*
[20] Short, M. *op. cit.,* 290
[21] Short, M. *ibid.* .91f. and Dickens, C., *op. cit.,* 409ff.
[22] Barth, K., *Dogmatics in Outline*, 30-34
[23] To explore further the question of constative and performative speech acts, see Sperber and Wilson, *Relevance: Communication and Cognition*, 243, Austin, J. L., *How To Do Things With Words* and Searle, J. R., *Expression and Meaning*, 12-20

BIBLIOGRAPHY

A: Primary Sources

Bennett, A. (1936 [1902]) *Anna of the Five Towns*. Harmondsworth: Penguin.

Carr, J. L. (1980) *A Month in the Country*. Harmondsworth: Penguin.

Eliot, G. (2008 [1859]) *Adam Bede*. Harmondsworth: Penguin Classics.

Hobbs, P. (2005) *The Short Day Dying*. London: Faber and Faber.

Hocking, J. (1933) *Not One in Ten*. London: Hodder and Stoughton.

Kaye-Smith, S. (1908) *The Tramping Methodist*. London: Cassell and Co. Ltd.

Quiller-Couch, A. (1908 [1903]) *Hetty Wesley*. London: J. M. Dent and Sons.

—. (1929 [1915]) *Nicky-Nan, Reservist*. London: J. M. Dent and Sons.

Spring, H. (1940) *Fame is the Spur*. London: Collins.

Unsworth, B. (2011) *The Quality of Mercy*. London: Hutchinson.

B: Other fiction, poetry and plays

Arditti, M. (2001) *Easter*. London: Arcadia Books.

Bashford, H. H. (1924) *Augustus Carp, Esq. by Himself*. London: Prion.

Bawden, N. (1973) *Carrie's War*. Harmondsworth: Penguin.

Brontë, A. (1988 [1847]) *Agnes Grey*. Harmondsworth: Penguin.

—. (1996 [1848]) *The Tenant of Wildfell Hall*. Harmondsworth: Penguin.

Brontë, C. (2006 [1847]) *Jane Eyre*. Harmondsworth: Penguin.

Brontë, E. (2009 [1847]) *Wuthering Heights*. London: Heron Books, Williams Collins Sons.

Brook, R. (1997) *The Testimony of Taliesin Jones*. London: Flamingo.

Chaplin, S. (1961) *The Day of the Sardine*. London: Eyre and Spottiswoode.

—. (1970) *The Leaping Lad*. London: Longman.

—. (1987) *In Blackberry Time*. Newcastle upon Tyne: Bloodaxe Books.

Crabbe, G. (1810) *The Borough: A Poem in 24 Letters*. Philadelphia: Bradford and Inskeep.

Davies, S. (2013) *Awakening*. London: Parthian.

Fielding, H. (1999 [1741]) *Shamela*. Harmondsworth: Penguin.

—. (2012 [1742]) *Joseph Andrews*. Harmondsworth: Penguin.

—. (2005 [1749]) *Tom Jones.* Harmondsworth: Penguin.
—. (1983 [1751]) *Amelia.* Oxford: Clarendon Press.
Frederic, H. (1896) *The Damnation of Theron Ware or Illumination.* Harmondsworth: Penguin.
Golding, W. (1954) *Lord of the Flies.* London: Faber and Faber.
Graves, R. (1967 [1773]) *The Spiritual Quixote, or the Summer's Ramble of Mr Geoffrey Wildgoose.* Oxford: Oxford University Press.
Hocking, S. K. (1879) *Her Benny.* London: Frederick Warne.
Melville, H. (2013 [1851]) *Moby-Dick.* London: Collins Classics.
Milton, J. (1956) *Poems.* London: Dent.
Murdoch, I. (1958) *The Bell.* London: Chatto and Windus.
—. (1966) *The Time of the Angels.* Harmondsworth: Penguin.
—. (1983) *The Philosopher's Pupil.* London: Chatto and Windus.
—. (1987) *The Book and the Brotherhood.* London: Chatto and Windus.
Smollett, T. (2008 [1771]) *The Expedition of Humphrey Clinker.* Harmondsworth: Penguin.
Sterne, L. (1927 [1744]) *The Sermons of Mr. Yorick Volume 1.* Oxford: Basil Blackwell.
Wright, D. (1978) *The Selected Poems of Thomas Hardy.* Harmondsworth: Penguin.

C: Secondary criticism

Alter, R. (2002) *Canon and Creativity: Modern Writing and the Authority of Scripture.* New Haven, Conn.: Yale University Press.
Anderson, B. (1991) *Imagined Communities.* New York: Verso.
Anderson, M. G. (2012) *Imagining Methodism in 18th-century Britain: Enthusiasm, Belief and the Borders of Self.* Baltimore: John Hopkins University Press.
Ashton, R. (2014) "Lunch with the Rector", *Times Literary Supplement* 5783, 15.
Augustine, (1961) *Confessions.* Harmondsworth: Penguin.
Austin, J. L. (1975) *How to do Things with Words.* Cambridge, Mass: Harvard University Press.
Bakhtin, M. M. (1981) *The Dialogical Imagination: Four Essays.* Austin: University of Texas Press, ET Michael Holquist.
—. (1986) "The Problem of Speech Genres", *Speech Genres and Other Essays.* Austin: University of Texas Press, 60-102, ET Michael Holquist.
Barth, K. (1949) *Dogmatics in Outline.* London: SCM Press.
Bauman, R. (1977) *Verbal Art as Performance.* Illinois: Waveland Press.

Booth, W. (1961) *The Rhetoric of Fiction.* Chicago: University of Chicago Press.

Brett, M. (2004) "In the English Lower Depths: Sid Chaplin's Newcastle Novels", *Times Literary Supplement* December 10, 21-22.

Brown, C. (2001) *The Death of Christian Britain: Understanding Secularisation 1800-2000.* London: Routledge.

Brown, P. and S. C. Levinson (1978) "Universals in Language Usage: politeness phenomena", *Questions and Politeness: Strategies in Social Interaction.* E. N. Goody, (ed.), Cambridge: Cambridge University Press, 256-289.

Brueggemann, W. (1989) *Finally Comes the Poet: Daring Speech for Proclamation.* Minneapolis: Fortress Press.

—. (1993) *The Bible and the Postmodern Imagination: Texts Under Negotiation.* London: SCM.

—. (1997) *Cadences of Home: Preaching among Exiles.* Louisville: Westminster John Knox Press.

—. (2000) *Deep Memory, Exuberant Hope: Contested Truth in a Post-Christian World.* Minneapolis: Fortress.

Burke, K. (1961) *The Rhetoric of Religion: Studies in Logology.* Boston: Beacon Press.

Burman, E. and I. Parker (1993) *Discourse Analytic Research: Repertoires and Readings of Texts in Action.* London: Routledge.

Butler, J. (1993) *Bodies that Matter: On the Discursive Limits of 'Sex'.* London: Routledge.

—. (1999) *Gender Trouble: Feminism and the Subversion of Identity.* London: Routledge.

Buttrick, D. (1987) *Homiletic.* Philadelphia: Fortress Press

Brooks, P. (2005) *Realist Vision.* Yale: Yale University Press.

Campbell, K. K. (1996) *The Rhetorical Act.* Belmont: Wordsworth Publishing.

Cash, A. H. (1964) "The Sermon in *Tristram Shandy*", *ELH* (31), 395-417.

Childers, J. (1998) *Performing the Word: Preaching as Theatre.* Nashville: Abingdon Press.

Church, L. F. (1949) *The Early Methodist People.* Peterborough: Epworth Press.

Compier, D. H. (1999) *What is Rhetorical Theology? Textual Practice and Public Discourse.* Pennsylvania: Trinity Press.

Conradi, P. J. (1989) *Iris Murdoch: The Saint and the Artist.* London: Macmillan.

—. (2001) *The Saint and the Artist: A Study of the Fiction of Iris Murdoch.* London: HarperCollins Publishers.

Cook, G. (1994) *Discourse and Literature*. Oxford: Oxford University Press.

Craske, J and C. Marsh, (1999) *Methodism and the Future: Facing the Challenge*. London: Cassell.

Culler, J. (2004) "Omniscience", *Narrative* 12 (1), 22-34.

Cunningham, D. S. (1990) *Faithful Persuasion: In Aid of a Rhetoric of Christian Theology*. London: University of Notre Dame Press.

Cunningham, V. (1975) *Everywhere Spoken Against: Dissent in the Victorian Novel.* Oxford: Clarendon Press.

Cupitt, D. (1991) *What is a Story?* London: SCM Press.

Currie, R. (1977) *Churches and Churchgoers: Patterns of Church Growth in the British Isles since 1700.* Oxford: Oxford University Press.

Davies, R., A. R. George and G. Rupp (eds.) (1978) *A History of the Methodist Church in Great Britain Volume 2.* Peterborough: Epworth Press.

Davies, R. (1976) *Methodism.* Peterborough: Epworth Press.

—. (1988) *What Methodists Believe.* Peterborough: Epworth Press.

Dickinson, D. (2007) "Troubled Preachers: Keeping the Faith", *Homiletic,* 32 (2), 1-10.

—. (2012) "Methodism in English Fiction", *International Journal for the Study of the Christian Church,* 12 (3-4), 309-323.

—. (2013) *The Novel as Church: Preaching to Readers in Contemporary Fiction.* Waco: Baylor University Press.

Drummond, A. L. (1950) "The Sermon in Victorian Fiction", *The Churches in English Fiction: A Literary and Historical Study, from the Regency to the Present Time, of British and American Fiction.* Leicester: Edgar Backus, 308-317.

Eagleton, T. (2005) *The English Novel: An Introduction.* Oxford: Blackwell.

Elam, K. (1980) *The Semiotics of Theatre and Drama.* London: Routledge.

Ellison, R. H. (1998) *The Victorian Pulpit: Spoken and Written Sermons in Nineteenth-century Britain.* London: Associated Universities Press.

Fabb, N. (1997) *Linguistics and Literature.* Oxford: Blackwell.

Ferretter, L. (2003) *Towards a Christian Literary Theory.* Basingstoke: Palgrave Macmillan.

Fiddes, P. (1999) *The Novel, Spirituality and Modern Culture.* Cardiff: University of Wales Pres.

Fish, S. (1994) *Is there a text in this class? The Authority of Interpretive Communities.* London: Harvard University Press.

Foucault, M. (1969) "What is an Author?", *Language, Counter-memory, Practice: Selected Essays and Interviews.* Donald B. Bouchard,(ed.). New York: Cornell University Press.

—. (1997) "Nietzsche, Genealogy, History", *The Foucault Reader: An Introduction to Foucault's Thought.* P. Rabinow, (ed.). Harmondsworth: Penguin, 76-100.

Gates, H. L. (1986) *The Signifying Monkey: A Theory of African-American Literary Criticism.* Oxford: Oxford University Press.

Gerhart, M. (1992) *Genre Choices, Genre Questions.* London: University of Oklahoma Press.

Gilmore, A. (1996) *Preaching as Theatre.* London: SCM.

Goody, E. N. (1978) *Questions and Politeness: Strategies in Social Interaction.* Cambridge: Cambridge University Press.

Gordon, E. (2012) "The author of *The Short Day Dying* who unexpectedly became a writer during a long illness", *The New Statesman.* http://www.newstatesman.com/books/2008/03/hobbs-sentimentality

Green, S. J. D. (2011) *The Passing of Protestant England: Secularisation and Social Change c.1920-1960.* Cambridge: Cambridge University Press.

Harrison, G. E. (1937) *Haworth Parsonage: A Study of the Wesleys and the Brontës.* Peterborough: Epworth.

—. (1948) *The Clue to the Brontës.* London: Methuen.

Herbst, M. T. (2007) "The Pernicious Effects of Novel Reading: The Methodist Episcopal Campaign against American Fiction, 1865-1914", *The Journal of Religion and Society* (9), 1-15.

Hindmarsh, D. B., (2005) *The Evangelical Conversion Narrative: Spiritual autobiography in early modern England.* Oxford: Oxford University Press.

Hobson, T. (2002) *The Rhetorical Word: Protestant Theology and the Rhetoric of Authority.* Aldershot: Ashgate.

Hogan, L. L. and R. Reid, (1999) *Connecting with the Congregation: Rhetoric and the Art of Preaching.* Nashville: Abingdon Press.

Hymes, D. (1974) *Foundations in Sociolinguistics: An Ethnographic Approach.* Philadelphia: University of Philadelphia Press.

James, H. (1914) "The New Novel", *Henry James: Literary Criticism vol. 1,* 129-133.

Kearns, M. (1999) *Rhetorical Narratology.* London: University of Nebraska Press.

Kennedy, G. A. (1980) *Classical Rhetoric and its Christian and Secular Traditions from Ancient to Modern Times.* London: Croom Helm.

Kent, A. M. (2002) *Pulp Methodism: The Lives and Literature of Silas, Joseph and Salome Hocking, Three Cornish Novelists.* Cornish Hillside Publications: St Austell.

Kinneavy, J. L. (1971) *A Theory of Discourse*. New Jersey: Prentice Hall.

Kitcher, P. (2014) *Life after Faith: The Case for Secular Humanism.* London: Yale University Press.

Knight, M. and T. Woodman (2006) *Biblical Religion and the Novel, 1700-1900.* Aldershot: Ashgate.

Lawson-Tancred, H. C. (1991) *Aristotle: The Art of Rhetoric.* Harmondsworth: Penguin Classics.

Leah, G. (2010) "'There your heart will be...' Thoughts on Covenant in the light of Peter Hobbs's Novel, *The Short Day Dying", Epworth Review* 37 (1), 18-27.

Leith, D and G. Myerson, (1989) *The Power of Address: Explorations in Rhetoric*. London: Routledge.

Lose, D. J. (2003) *Confessing Jesus Christ: Preaching in a Postmodern World*. Cambridge: William B Eerdmans Publishing.

Lyotard, J-F. (1984) *The Postmodern Condition: A Report on Knowledge.* Manchester: Manchester University Press.

Martin, D. (2014) *Religion and Power: No Logos without Mythos.* Farnham: Ashgate.

Matz, J. (2004) *The Modern Novel: A Short Introduction.* Oxford: Blackwell Publishing.

McConnell, J. E. (2007) "The Character of Methodism in George Eliot's *Adam Bede*", *Methodist History* (45:4), 244-253.

Merrill, T. (1976) *Christian Criticism: A Study of Literary God-Talk.* Amsterdam: Rodopi.

Miles, R. (2000) "John Wesley as Interreligious Resource: Would You Take This Man to an Interfaith Dialogue?", M. Forward, S. Plant and S. White (eds.) *A Great Commission: Christian Hope and Religious Diversity.* Bern: Peter Lang.

Miller, L. P. (1978) "Casting Graven Images: *The Damnation of Theron Ware*", *Renascence: Essays on Values in Literature.* (30), 178-184.

Myers, R. M. (1994) "Antimodern Protest in *The Damnation of Theron Ware*", *American Literary Realism* (26:3), 52-64.

Nash, J. and B. S. Suess, (2001) *New Approaches to the Literary Art of Anne Brontë*. Aldershot: Ashgate.

Ogawa, K. (2012) "Religious Sensibility in Anne Brontë's *Agnes Grey* and *The Tenant of Wildfell Hall*", *Bulletin of the Faculty of Foreign Studies, Sophia University* (47), 1-21.

Olson, D. R. and N. Torrance, (1991) *Literacy and Orality*. Cambridge: Cambridge University Press.

Ong, W. J. (1982) *Orality and Literacy: The Technologizing of the Word*. London: Routledge.

Parrinder, G. (1992) "The Great Novelist of English Religion", *Epworth Review* (19:3) 79-87.

Parrinder, P. (2006) *Nation and Novel: The English Novel from its Origins to the Present Day*. Oxford: Oxford University Press.

Plumstead. A.W. (ed.) (1968) *The Wall and the Garden: Selected Massachusetts Election Sermons, 1670-1775*. Minnesota: Minnesota University Press.

Pope, R. (2002) *The English Studies Book: An Introduction to Language, Literature and Culture*. London: Routledge.

Potter, J. and M. Wetherell, (1987) *Discourse and Social Psychology: Beyond Attitudes and Behaviour*. London: Sage Publications.

Price Hughes, D. (1916) "The Novels of Mr Arnold Bennett and Wesleyan Methodism", *Contemporary Review* (Nov.) 602-610.

Prickett, S. (ed.) (2014) *The Edinburgh Companion to the Bible and the Arts*. Edinburgh: Edinburgh University Press.

Quiller-Couch, A. (1944) *Memories and Opinions of Q: An Unfinished Autobiography*. Roberts, S.C. (ed.) Cambridge: Cambridge University Press.

Richter, P. and L. Francis, (1998) *Gone But Not Forgotten*. London: Darton, Longman and Todd.

Ricoeur, P. (1978) *The Rule of Metaphor: Multi-disciplinary studies of the creation of meaning in language*. London: Routledge and Kegan Paul.

—. (1979) "The Function of Fiction in Shaping Reality", *Man and World* (12) 123-141.

Rivers I. (1978) "Strangers and Pilgrims: Sources and Patterns of Methodist Narrative", *Augustan Worlds*. Hilson, J.D., Jones, M.M.B. and Watson, J.R., (eds.) Leicester: Leicester University Press, 189-203.

Robertson, D. W. (1958) *St Augustine on Christian Doctrine*. New York: Macmillan.

Rzepka, C. and J. Rzepka, (2000) "Seeing into the life of things", *Moral Cross-dressing: Contemporary Trends in Liberal Preaching and Literary Criticism*. Mahoney, J., ed., Fordham University Press, 88-107.

Scotland, N. A. D. (1997) "Methodism and the English Labour Movement 1800-1906", *Anvil.* (14.1), 36-48.

Searle, J. R. (1979) *Expression and Meaning: Studies in the Theory of Speech Acts*. Cambridge: Cambridge University Press.

Shepherd, T. B. (1940) *Methodism and the Literature of the Eighteenth Century.* London: Epworth.

Short, M. (1996) *Exploring the Language of Poems, Plays and Prose.* Harlow: Longman.

Simpson, P. (1993) *Language, Ideology and Point of View.* London: Routledge.

—. (1997) *Language through Literature: An Introduction.* London: Routledge.

Smith, F. L. (1993) "The Pulpit and Woman's Place: Gender and the Framing of the 'Exegetical Self' in Sermon Performances", *Framing in Discourse* ed. D. Tannen. Oxford: Oxford University Press.

Soskice, J. M. (1985) *Metaphor and Religious Language.* Oxford: Clarendon Press.

Sperber, D. and D. Wilson, (1986) *Relevance: Communication and Cognition.* Oxford: Blackwell.

Spring, M. H. (1967) *Howard.* London: Collins.

Stockwell, P. (2001) *Cognitive Poetics: An Introduction.* London: Routledge.

Stout, H. S. (1991) *The Divine Dramatist: George Whitefield and the Rise of Modern Evangelicalism.* Grand Rapids: Eerdmans.

Swales, J. M. (1990) *Genre Analysis: English in Academic and Research Settings.* Cambridge: Cambridge University Press.

Tannen, D. (1994) *Talking from 9 to 5: Women and Men at Work: Language, sex and power.* London: Virago.

Tate, A. (2008) *Contemporary Fiction and Christianity.* London: Continuum.

Taylor, C. (2007) *A Secular Age.* Cambridge, Mass.: Harvard University Press.

Tew, P. (2004) *The Contemporary British Novel.* London: Continuum.

Tew, P. and R. Mengham, (eds.), (2006) *British Fiction Today.* London: Continuum.

Tillich, H. (1974) *From Time to Time.* London: George Allen & Unwin.

Tillich, P. (1951) *Systematic Theology Volume 1.* London: SCM Press.

—. (1957) *Systematic Theology Volume 2: Existence and the Christ.* London: SCM Press.

—. (1959) *Theology of Culture.* New York: Oxford University Press.

Todorov, T. (1990) *Genres in Discourse.* Cambridge: Cambridge University Press.

Toolan, M. J. (1988) *Narrative: A Critical Linguistic Introduction.* London: Routledge.

Toulmin, S. (1958) *The Uses of Argument*. Cambridge: Cambridge University Press.

Trustees for Methodist Church Purposes, (1983) *Hymns and Psalms*. Peterborough: Methodist Publishing House.

—. (1999) *The Methodist Worship Book*. Peterborough: Methodist Publishing House.

—. (2011) *Singing the Faith*. London: Hymns Ancient and Modern.

Turner, J. M. (1998) *Modern Methodism in England 1932-1998*. Peterborough: Epworth Press.

Wakefield, G. S. (1999) *Methodist Spirituality*. Peterborough: Epworth Press.

Walsh, C. (2001) *Gender and Discourse: Language and Power in Politics, the Church and Organisations*. London: Longman.

Williams, Raymond, (1977) *Marxism and Literature*. Oxford: Oxford University Press.

Williams, Rowan, (2012) *Faith in the Public Square*. London: Bloomsbury.

Winchester, C.T. (1905) "Methodism in the Light of the Literature of the Last Century by J. Albert Swallow Review", *The Journal of English and German Philology*. (5:3), 372-374.

Wood, J. (2015) *The Nearest Thing to Life*. London: Jonathan Cape.

Worton, M. and J. Still, (1990) *Intertextuality: Theories and Practices*. Manchester: Manchester University Press.

Zimmerman, D. H. (1994) "Clay Feet, Modernism and Fundamental Option in Harold Frederic's *The Damnation of Theron Ware*", *The American Benedictine Review*. (45.1), 33-44.

INDEX